BLOODY BRITISH HISTORY

LIVERPOOL

KEN PYE

The
History
Press

The History Press
The Mill, Brimscombe Port
Stroud, Gloucestershire, GL5 2QG
www.thehistorypress.co.uk

Reprinted 2012, 2013

British Library Cataloguing in Publication Data.
A catalogue record for this book is available from the British Library.

ISBN 978 0 7524 6551 7

Typesetting and origination by The History Press
Printed and bound by TJ International Ltd, Padstow, Cornwall

CONTENTS

INTRODUCTION

THE RECORDED HISTORY of Liverpool only goes back for around 800 years. In fact, the town does not even appear in William the Conqueror's Domesday Book of 1086 – that great ledger of his new territories and properties, and of everything that he could extract a tax from.

But Liverpudlians, in one form or another, have been around for much longer than that!

Through all the major eras of ancient British history, we have played our part, and we have always had major significance. Yet it was not until 1715 that the fortunes of Liverpool began to change. This was the year that the world's first commercial wet-dock opened in the town. The 'New Dock', as it was called, was created by reclaiming the large, tidal inlet off the River Mersey, known as 'The Pool' – and which gave the medieval town its name.

Within fifty years we were already becoming the most important city and port in the British Empire, outside London, a position we were to hold well into the twentieth century.

Throughout the centuries we have achieved much; and our scientists, merchants, artists, poets, economists, educators and musicians have helped change the face of the globe. Liverpool is known all around that globe, because of those achievements.

But there has been a darker side to our history too: sometimes of our own making, and sometimes as victims of fate or foe. It is that story that I shall tell in this book.

From those prehistoric Liverpudlians through to the wars of the twentieth century there are terrible tales to tell – and the best ones are in the following pages.

Ken Pye
Liverpool, 2011

55BC

THE FIRST FEARSOME 'SCOUSERS'

Druidical Sacrifice and Naked Blue Natives

STONE AGE MAN probably had settlements on the banks of the River Mersey, as in all likelihood did Bronze Age peoples. That the Iron Age Celts were here is certain – the first 'Scousers'. Tribes fought each other for power and territory, but they banded together with determined and dedicated brutality against any enemy – and some of those foes were powerful indeed.

The Romans first attempted to invade Britain in 55BC, under the command of Julius Caesar. He attacked the Kent coast with ninety-eight ships and two legions; each of 20,000 men. The response from the native Britons was severe and brutal, and he was soon repelled. But this was only a temporary reprieve – Caesar had his sights set on our rich resources: wheat, copper, tin, lead, silver, gold, and slaves.

Caesar's next attack was the following year. This time he was better prepared; he attacked the east coast of Britain with 800 ships, 50,000 soldiers, and 2,000 cavalry. Caesar conquered the south-eastern Celtic tribes but left again, three months later, with his entire army.

The Romans did not come back again until AD 43; but this time they were under the command of Emperor Claudius.

He was absolutely determined to subjugate the country, and its wild, warrior, Celtic inhabitants – no matter what the cost in time or men. And it took decades, because the tribespeople put up a ferocious defence. In fact, it was not until around AD 70–79 that he got to the north-west of England – hacking, slashing, spearing, mutilating, impaling, and beheading every step of the way. He left the heads of the beaten Celtic Chieftains stuck on pikes, as a warning to others.

These were times of magic and mystery in ancient Britain, and of a human relationship with the earth, the skies, the waters, and the natural world that has long since vanished. Even today, legends abound of the mysterious Druids – the priestly cult that seems to have been at the very pinnacle of Celtic society in those dark and bloodthirsty times. For many years these stories were thought to be nothing but Roman propaganda, but recent archaeological finds now lead scientists to believe that perhaps the Druids really did exist, and were indeed a bloodthirsty sect.

The usual picture is of bearded, white-robed mystics, harvesting mistletoe with golden sickles to use in strange rites; and of naked dances, held under the moon and

The Emperor Claudius.

stars in groves of sacred oak trees. Stories of mass human executions inside the dreaded 'Wicker Man' abound.

Julius Caesar himself described how hapless victims would be imprisoned in gigantic wooden cages, fashioned out of woven branches to look like human figures. Fires would be lit at the feet of these timber manikins, and the agonised screams of the men, women, and children, as they slowly roasted alive, would soon be swallowed up in the black smoke, raging heat, and sheets of orange and red flames. Sometimes, live cattle and other animals would be burned with the people, only adding to the horror of the ritual.

Yarns persist too of ceremonial human sacrifice on great carved slabs, set in circles of standing stones. Such tales circulated in the late nineteenth century, in what are now the southern suburbs of Liverpool, near Woolton Village, when archaeologists

investigated six irregular sandstone slabs. For generations known by local people as the 'Calder Stones', the scientists declared them to be remnants of a 'Druidical Stone Circle'. This was reinforced by the fact that the word 'Calder' is derived from the Anglo-Saxon 'Galdar' or 'Wizard' – so the belief was that bloody sacrifices were carried out in ancient Liverpool!

Druids may well have practised their ceremonies here, but the Calder Stones are now known to have been the remnants of a chambered tomb – part of a long-vanished Neolithic chief's tumulus. This had originally been erected around 4,800BC, therefore making it older even than Stonehenge (built around 3100BC) – which itself is older than the first Pyramids of Egypt (begun around 2600BC). We Scousers have been around for a very long time!

The Iron Age Britons fiercely defended their homes, communities, and lands – especially in what was to become Liverpool and Merseyside. There is little local evidence of these ancient inhabitants of our area but, at the top of the 250ft high Camp Hill, close to Woolton Village, the same

Druids and arch druids.

Stonehenge: Liverpool's Caldar Stones are even more ancient than this site.

Victorian archaeologists also discovered the remains of a large Iron Age fort, or 'camp'.

Named as a consequence of this discovery, Camp Hill had been occupied by a local tribe of Brigantes. This confederation of largely independent communities controlled the largest section of what would become Northern England, and a significant part of the Midlands. They had constructed this defensive outpost to protect their surrounding farms and fields.

The fortification was around 80 yards in diameter, with ramparts between 10ft and 15ft high, and probably encircled by defensive, sharpened wooden stakes. From the top of Camp Hill, even today, the views of the surrounding lands, the River Mersey, the Wirral Peninsular, and the far mountains of North Wales are spectacular, so this was an ideal location for the competitive local Celts. They would have challenged other local tribes for power and

territory from here, and defended themselves against the Romans when they came.

And evidence shows that they did indeed come here; by river and by land. In the early 2000s, when the foundations of what would become the new, city-centre retail complex, 'Liverpool ONE', were being excavated, the remnants of a Roman galleon were discovered, on the site of the original tidal pool that gave the city its name.

The Roman invaders also probably marched past Camp Hill, on the way from their northern base at Bremetennacum – now modern Ribchester – to Deva – the city now known as Chester. And, in the mid-nineteenth century, during road excavations in nearby Garston, the remains of a Roman pavement were discovered below the roadway.

The Brigantean hillfort would have been a prime target for the invading Romans,

One of the other methods of ritual execution and sacrifice used by the Druids was 'the Threefold Death'.

Victims would be held under water until they almost drowned; then they were hanged to within an inch of death. Finally, they were cut down and mortally wounded – to eventually, and painfully, bleed to death.

and it is also probable that they would have mounted at least one attack against its pre-historic Scouse defenders. It is believed that Gaius Julius Agricola (Governor of Britain from AD 78 to 84) led major attacks against the Brigantes – although it took many years to finally conquer them. Even early Liverpudlians were taken on at peril!

The Romans reported too that their Celtic enemies often fought entirely naked – their bodies painted all over, or in swirling patters, with blue woad extracted from plants. I can imagine the Romans, in their burnished armour, ready with their spears and broadswords, lined up at the base of the rise in serried and orderly ranks.

I can visualise, too, the daunting spectacle of hundreds of naked, powerful, angry, hairy blue men (and sometimes the women as well) gathered at the top of Camp Hill. Also heavily armed, with fearsome, long and slender slashing swords and vicious spears, they would charge screaming down the hill. Throwing themselves against the enemy in furious abandon, the effect that these rampant early Scousers had on the invaders can only be imagined.

But the Romans were not the only ruthless invaders that the early people of Liverpool had to contend with – far from it.

AD 800

THE TERROR FROM THE NORTH

The Bloodthirsty Vikings of Merseyside

IN AD 410, the Emperor Honorious withdrew all Romans from Britain, telling the country that we now had to fend for ourselves. The Dark Ages had begun.

Now, other warlike peoples from Europe set their sights on the land across the channel, and for the same reasons that had originally brought the Romans here. Over subsequent centuries we were to be invaded and settled by the Angles, the Saxons, and the Jutes – all adding to the cultural mix that was to evolve into Anglo-Saxon Britain. But then, from the ninth century onwards, a race of new, sea-born aggressors began to invade our shores – this time from Scandinavia.

Coming here in fleets of 'longships', driven by sails, oars, and a bloodthirsty determination to conquer, Norse warriors such as 'Eric Bloodaxe' and 'Ivar the Boneless' would write the next chapter in Britain's bloody history – especially in north-west England and the ancient territories that were to become Merseyside.

Strong, proud, and relentless; with as many as 100 men in each vessel, they sailed across the icy and treacherous North Sea. Seated on benches on open decks, they were completely exposed to the elements; these Viking raiders were fearsome indeed. Their wooden warships were steered by a single oar at the rear and could be up to 36 metres in length. The prows and sterns were surmounted by awesome figureheads carved in the form of great dragons and monsters, designed to strike terror in to their enemies as they approached the land. Travelling at up to 10 or 11 knots, these were powerful vessels.

The ships' narrow beam and shallow draught meant that they could sail far inland up British rivers and broader streams. They could also plough directly onto shale and sand shorelines, or anchor very close to shore – right in the very heart of the settlements and communities that were their target.

These 'Norsemen' were from Sweden, Denmark, and Norway, and would strike with terrible violence and then rapidly move on, before any local defensive force could muster. Raids by single longships were frequent, but fleets of up to 100 ships could mount a single attack. As the Vikings became more familiar with our geography – and bolder as a result – fleets of up to 200 ships would be sighted approaching the land. Horrified observers would run to warn people – but often to no avail.

Invaders from the sea! Viking reached Liverpool in the ninth century.

When their objective was in sight – be it monastery, village, farm, or manor – the invaders would leap ashore over the shield-decorated sides of their ships and immediately go into frenzied and bloodthirsty attacks. Armed with saxes (single-edge swords), bows and arrows, spears, halberds (long blades mounted on short poles), and great battle-axes, when the Norsemen engaged with their victims they were ruthless.

Any person was fair game, regardless of sex, age, or social standing. Monks and nuns could expect no leniency either, and murder, mutilation, rape, and plunder were the frequent outcome of a Viking attack. All could expect to fall victim to these terrifying and vicious warriors – only the lucky few escaped to tell the tale and spread news of the horror.

Vikings seldom wore armour over their heavy fur and woollen clothing; possibly only leather tunics and – much more rarely – chain mail. But they did wear metal, bowl-shaped helmets – often with nose or face guards, but never with horns sticking out of them! They carried circular shields made of oak or other dense timber, and with heavy, raised bosses. They used these as deadly blunt instruments – pounding them into faces and breaking skulls.

The first Viking attack on Britain came in the year AD 793, when they sacked the Northumbrian monastery at Lindisfarne, sending a wave of shock, outrage, and fear across Western Europe. These determined people now regarded the rest of Britain as a legitimate target for looting and despoiling. The first raid by the Vikings on mainland England was recorded in Wessex in AD 855, but then they also targeted Ireland, Scotland, Wales, and Cornwall.

However, the Danes specifically set their sights on north-east and north-western England, and they were the race who exploited and subjugated the Liverpool and Merseyside areas of that time. Their first landing points in our scattered, rural villages were at what is now Crosby, just north of modern Liverpool, and at Meols, on the Wirral peninsular. A wide variety of Norse artefacts continue to be discovered at both of these coastal locations.

The Vikings voyaged far from their cold and often hostile homelands in the north, being driven by a lack of good farmlands, to seek new territory to plunder and then to settle. Even though, over the next 100 years, their attacks became more frequent and widespread throughout the British Isles, like other invaders before them, the Vikings were really only looking for new places in which to set up home. The Norsemen sailed their longboats up the River Mersey, the Alt, and the Dee,

and they settled here, in the Liverpool and north Cheshire areas, in significant numbers.

But the Vikings did not have it all their own way – especially when it came to taking on our hardy Merseyside ances-tors. They met their match, in no uncertain terms, at the Battle of Brunanburh, in AD 937.

In *The Anglo-Saxon Chronicle*, written throughout this period and recording events by contemporary writers and scribes, a poem recites the gory details of the battle, saying, 'Never yet on this island has there been a greater slaughter'.

Many historians now suggest that Brunanburh was, in fact, Bromborough on the Wirral, which once had a Scandi-navian colony. It has been said that 'true Englishness was born' during this terrible battle. This was because, for the first time

After a Viking attack: monks, nuns, women and children – all could expect no mercy.

Norse sagas tell of a particular kind of Viking warrior whose superhuman strength, ferociousness, and dedication to relentless slaughter was believed to be the manifestation of special magical powers. Their uncontrollable violence was frenzied, and they would not stop until slaughter was complete. Often going into battle unarmed and screaming at their adversaries, they relied on brute force and terror to overcome their foe.

These were 'the Berserkers': a term we understand well, even today.

in recorded history, an army of Saxon tribes united to defend their communities and homeland against a massive force.

Under the leadership of Athelstan, King of Wessex and Alfred the Great's grandson, the Saxons lined up to face combined ranks of Viking soldiers and their Celtic Allies, under the command of King Olaf Guthfrithsson. Seven Earls and five Kings were amongst the Celtic dead, and many Saxons perished too, 'on the battlefield where banners crashed and spears clashed in that meeting of men, that weapon-wrestle... on the death-field.'

The resulting carnage was staggering: even the most war-hardened warriors taking part were shocked by the level of slaughter. Backwards and forwards across the battlefield the armies pressed until, finally, the Saxons gained the upper hand and cornered the Celts; giving no quarter, putting many to the sword, and forcing the rest to flee in terror and shame: 'The Northmen went off in nail-bound ships, sad survivors of spears... ashamed in their hearts.'

What remains of the battlefield is near Storeton Woods, overlooking a modern golf course. But today the open land reveals nothing of the chaos that left countless mutilated bodies staining the grass with their blood; now only food for 'the dusk-dressed one, the dark raven, with hard beak of horn, and the hoar-coated one, white-tailed eagle, enjoying the carrion, greedy war-hawk, and that grey beast, the wolf of the wood.'

Treaties were eventually agreed and hostilities ended, as the Norse invaders eventually settled and married into the local Anglo-Saxon communities. They soon gave up their former warrior ways to become farmers and merchants.

Vikings now helped to establish new communities whilst strengthening and developing older ones. We see this legacy all around us on modern Merseyside, in the names of our suburbs, villages, and towns, such as Ormskirk, Kirkby, Fazakerley, Garston, Toxteth, Hale, and Knowsley.

But, on that day in AD 937, in ancient Bromborough, the Anglo-Saxon nation was truly born.

BAD KING JOHN, THE FOUNDER OF LIVERPOOL

Of Stocks, Pillories and Cucking Stools

ONLY **129 YEARS** after the Battle of Brunanburh, England was to fall prey, once again, to an invader from over the seas. However, this time the country's subjugation was total, and to an extent that even the Romans had never achieved – this was our invasion and conquest, in 1066, by the Norman French.

William of Normandy (*c.* 1028–1087) – 'The Conqueror' – planned to completely obliterate everything Anglo-Saxon that he could – the language, customs, way of worship, legal system, and the social structures. He replaced this with the strict ranking of the feudal system, and England would never be the same again.

Life under successive Plantagenet monarchs was harsh and brutal, not least of all under King John (1167–1216). Said to have been a selfish, spoilt, sullen, and vindictive man, who was given to childish tantrums, he has passed into popular history as 'Bad King John'. Greedy, ruthless, and most certainly not to be trusted, John even murdered young hostages he was holding prisoner. These included his twenty-year-old nephew, Duke Arthur of Brittany, whom he had kept in a deep dungeon until, in a drunken rage, the King tied rocks to the young man and pushed him into a river to drown.

In 1210, King John captured Maud de Braose and her eldest son, William. They were transported to Windsor Castle in cages and later moved to Corfe Castle. Here, John had them walled up alive in a dungeon to starve to death. In 1212, the belligerent monarch hanged twenty-eight sons of Welsh princes and lords whom he was holding hostage, including 'an excellent boy not yet seven years old'.

However, John was seldom successful in battle, earning himself the nickname of 'Softsword' – which did not only belittle his prowess on a battlefield! When he came to the throne, in 1199, he had inherited a vast empire in France, but by the time of his death he had lost most of this – earning himself another nickname, 'John Lackland'.

The people, and the aristocracy, were no longer prepared to put up with him, so the Barons rebelled and, in 1215, King John was forced to sign the Magna Carta, at Runnymede. This laid the foundations for our modern personal rights and freedoms.

John died from dysentery in 1216; few people mourned his passing. But he had done at least one remarkable thing – in 1207 he had founded Liverpool (or 'Leverpul', as it was then known).

By issuing 'Letters Patent' – or 'Charter' – the King created the Town and Borough of Leverpul, simply because he wanted a new base from which to invade Ireland. This tiny collection of fishermen's cottages was so insignificant that it is not even listed in the Domesday Book of 1086. Its large tidal inlet off the River Mersey – the pool that gave ancient 'Leverpul' its name – would provide a safe harbour for his invasion fleets. The great Toxteth forest, off the pool's southern shore, would supply the timber to build them. Little did John, or those medieval 'Liverpudlians', realise that this previously unimportant hamlet would gradually develop into the most wealthy and influential city and port in the British Empire outside London.

But that was a long time in the future, and the newly-created town of Liverpool now had to grow and develop under callous rulers, self-serving aristocrats and landowners, a rigorous social structure,

The Great Seal of King John.

and living conditions so harsh that we can scarcely imagine them.

The people needed to find diversion and amusement where they could, and these distractions reflected the cruelty and violence of the times. There were cockfights; roosters with sharp, curved spurs, fastened to their legs, would slash each other to death. Then there was the spectacle of bull and bear-baiting. Here, aggressive and deliberately starved dogs would be set

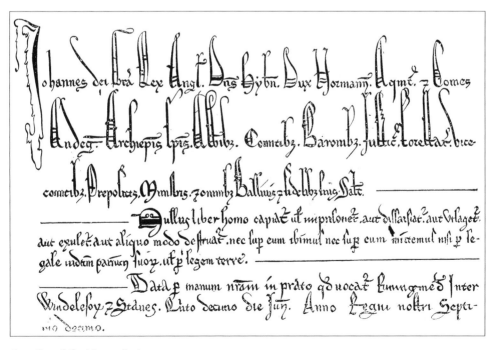

A section of the Magna Carta.

upon the larger animals, which would be chained or tethered to stakes. Unable to escape, they would be torn to pieces.

And medieval attitudes to life and death did not differentiate too much between the animal and human worlds, except that when people derived entertainment from the suffering of their fellows, this was done in the name of 'criminal justice'. Those found guilty of crimes were put in the stocks, or were pilloried, ducked, branded, or flogged, and these public punishments always drew big crowds: in Liverpool, as in every other community.

A hanging was an even better reason for a day out and a picnic, and the crowds that jeered around the cock-pits and bear-pits were much larger and even more vocal when they gathered to witness these slow strangulations.

Liverpool's first Town Hall was on Dale Street from 1515, and was known as the 'Exchange'. On its lowest level was the town gaol, but simply locking someone up provided no spectacle or entertainment. Nearby, however, and offering genuine 'audience participation', stood the town stocks and the pillory – both in frequent use. In fact, by 1351, every town in England was required by law to have and maintain a set of stocks.

Sitting on hard wooden benches, with ankles – and sometimes wrists – placed through holes in the horizontal wooden boards, the criminal in the stocks would find time passed extremely slowly. The stocks were used to punish crimes that were considered less serious. For swearing, the sentence was one hour; for drunkenness, up to six hours. Liverpool's court records of the time report that a 'naughtie person' was fined 2s 6d and sentenced to a period in the stocks for 'being sire of a bastard'.

For fraud, perjury, military desertion, or other significant but non-violent offences, a person could be locked in the stocks, continuously, for several days, being fed

———∞———

The last person to be pilloried in England was Peter James Bossy, in 1830. After being found guilty of perjury, he was offered either seven years' penal transportation or one hour in the pillory. He chose the pillory – and survived!

———∞———

The pillory, which forced a man to stand upright for hours at a time, and risk being maimed – or even killed – by the missiles that might be hurled at him.

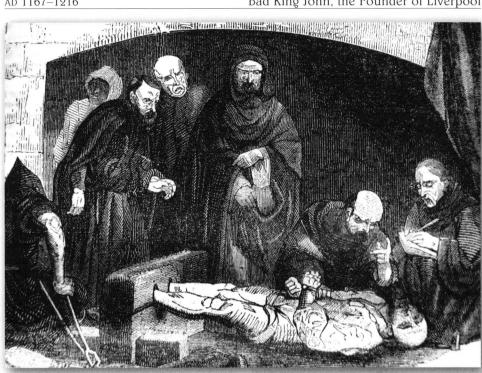

The stocks – as demonstrated, most horribly, by the Inquisition.

Dale Street in the early years of the twentieth century: still filled with municipal buildings four centuries after the first Town Hall was built on this site.

only bread and water. They could not move, even to relieve themselves. But spectators could, and frequently did, urinate or defecate on them.

If the worst you suffered was abuse, spitting, kicking, humiliation, and considerable physical discomfort, then you got off quite lightly: as this punishment took place in all weathers, victims could die of hypothermia or heatstroke. However, it could be much worse if you had to spend time in the pillory.

Here, with your head bent forward to be secured at the neck, together with your wrists, through holes in a hinged board, people were actively encouraged to throw missiles at you. Sometimes these would

One type of ducking stool; though variations in design were common, the same basic principle prevailed across the country.

only be mud, rotten vegetables, or manure, but they might often be sticks and stones, which did more than break bones; they could blind, permanently maim, or kill – all in the name of justice. The pillory was also used for flogging, branding, having your ears cut off, or your nostrils slit. And then there was ducking.

The ducking or 'cuck' stool was located near the 'Watering Place', on the corner of today's Crosshall Street and Hatton Garden, off Dale Street. This was used to punish wives and daughters who 'misbehaved', particularly those 'whose nagging became intolerable to their menfolk'.

The woman was forced to sit – often tied – in a chair, which was secured at one end of a long, thick pole. This was mounted on a tall pivot, like a see-saw, with the chair suspended over deep water, such as a pond. Men would use ropes attached to the other end of the pole to repeatedly raise and lower the victim into the pond, so that she was completely submerged in the often filthy and freezing water. She could be kept under water in this way for some time, frequently nearly drowning as a consequence.

It was a long time before such primitive punishments, and sources of public entertainment, fell into disuse: even as late as 1799, the ducking stool was used in the House of Correction, which had by then been built on Mount Pleasant, in the town.

Today we find our entertainment in ways that are less humiliating to our fellow man – or do we? What about *Big Brother; I'm a Celebrity....; The X Factor; Britain's Got Talent...*

'A HORSE! A HORSE! MY KINGDOM FOR A HORSE!'

Betrayal, Slaughter, Fame and Fortune

THE MEDIEVAL MONARCHS of England did not have it all their own way: throughout this period of history they suffered many challenges to their rule and authority. Some of these were more successful than others, and changed the course of English history as a result. Such is the story of King Richard III, and of Lord Thomas Stanley (1435?–1504), the man who was to become one of the Lords of Liverpool and founder of a dynasty that continues today.

In 1483, Richard, Duke of York (1452–1485), became the thirteenth English monarch after King John, and this unlucky number reflects the nature of his short reign. He was the last of the great Plantagenet ancestral line but, like his predecessor, has gone down in history with a very bad reputation.

When King Edward IV died, in 1483, Richard, who was his brother, had been named as Lord Protector of his nephew: the twelve-year-old was the new King, Edward V. But, as the boy-King was making his way to London, Richard met him and escorted him to the capital, where he placed him in apartments in the Tower. He was soon to be joined by his younger brother, also named Richard, but the two young boys were never seen again.

Rumours were rife then, and suspicions persist to this day, that Richard of York had the children murdered in the Tower. To this was added the fact that he declared that the Princes' mother, Elizabeth Woodville, had been illegally married to Edward IV. This made the boy-King's right to the throne invalid, so Richard claimed the Crown for himself.

Richard III.

19

In 1674, during alterations to the Tower of London, the skeletons of two children were discovered buried under some stone steps, 'at the stair-foot, meetly deep'. Believed to be the lost 'Princes in The Tower', murdered by their notorious uncle in 1483, the bones were placed in an urn and interred in Westminster Abbey.

Exhumed again, in 1933, and scientifically examined, they were then reburied: this time confirmed as Edward IV and his little brother, Prince Richard.

The Tower of London in the fifteenth century.

Because the new throne of King Richard III was set on very unstable foundations, opportunist rivals to his title saw their chance and mounted rebellions. The last, and most fateful, of these took place in August 1485. Henry Tudor (1457–1509), 2nd Earl of Richmond, landed unopposed at Mill Bay in Pembrokeshire, close to his Welsh birthplace. A direct descend-ant of the Welsh King, Rhys ap Gruffydd (1132–1197), Henry had brought with him an army of 5,000 soldiers, mostly mercenaries, and he now marched inland. Richard, with an army of between 8,000 and 10,000 men, was waiting for him near the small town of Market Bosworth, in Leicestershire, where he had taken a commanding position on a hilltop.

As battle was joined, the King was confident of victory – he had a superior force in numbers and armour – so his tactic was to separate his army into three phalanxes. One of these he commanded himself; the second was led by the Earl of Northumberland; and the third, by the Duke of Norfolk. Henry Tudor kept all his men together, determined to defeat 'the Yorkist usurper'. But Norfolk's battle group immediately launched themselves against Tudor's troops and, on foot and on horse, the conflict was bloody and without quarter.

Salvos of cannonfire criss-crossed the battlefield, wounding and killing hundreds. Then wave after wave of deadly arrows rained down, on men inadequately protected against this merciless hail. Horses ran down foot soldiers, but were themselves impaled on spears and hacked by swords. Knights in full armour clashed together, slicing and slashing at all around them, as the ordinary soldiers fought more for their own lives than for the victory of their leaders. Bodies began to form mounds on the battlefield, which began to turn from verdant green to bloody crimson, as the noise and stench of death swept across the scene.

Richard's army may have had the numbers, but they did not all have the will, or the courage, and some of his men deserted the battlefield. The King's position was now extremely vulnerable, and Richard felt that to charge directly at Henry Tudor was now a risk worth taking. He had seen that there were troops ranged under his banner who had not yet fully engaged in the battle, and whom he expected would rally to his call.

These soldiers belonged to Lord Thomas Stanley, and his brother, Sir William, and numbered around 5,000 men. Richard expected Stanley's support: he was holding Lord Thomas's son hostage to ensure it. But Thomas was married to the widowed mother of Henry Tudor, so his loyalty actually lay with his wife's family, and therefore with Henry, who was his stepson.

The Stanley's, who were wealthy and powerful landowners around South Lancashire, particularly in and around medieval Liverpool, had been deliberately waiting to see which way the battle was going before committing themselves to the fight: they had no intention of coming out on the losing side. But then Sir William Stanley saw King Richard battling his way towards Henry Tudor – pulling ahead of his own knights as he did so, and exposing himself to unprotected attack.

Whatever subsequent chroniclers may have written about Richard III, his reckless courage in the battle was beyond doubt. He charged ahead with his sword poised, ready to slay Henry. Richard decimated the pretender's bodyguard in the process, and killed Henry's standard bearer with a single sword thrust. But seeing the King now alone and separated from the rest of his army, the Stanleys made a decision that would seal the King's fate, and their own, and they finally made their move – but it wasn't to support Richard.

Seeing where the King's troops were most vulnerable, Sir William Stanley led his men to attack them from the rear. Lord Thomas Stanley led his men forward too,

The murder of the princes in the Tower on Richard III's orders.

21

Sir Thomas Stanley offers the crown to Henry Tudor on Bosworth Field.

but directly at the King. As Lord Thomas closed in on Richard, the King now realised his position and turned to face his new attacker. But Richard, and his few remaining knights, were surrounded and massively outnumbered by Stanley's men, who now pressed them towards a nearby marsh. Tradition has it that Richard was unhorsed, crying out, 'Treachery! Treachery! Treachery!' when he realised how the Stanleys had betrayed him.

There was indeed treachery at the Battle of Bosworth Field, but there was courage also. In this final skirmish the King's banner man, Sir Percival Thirwell, had both his legs hacked off. Even so, he remained in the saddle, holding the King's standard firmly aloft. But all was lost for Richard: his own men now deserted him, and William Shakespeare has the King, now on foot and desperately calling out, in his last moments, 'A horse, a horse; my kingdom for a horse!'

Completely surrounded and defeated, King Richard III was finally slain with a poleaxe, wielded by Tudor's man, Sir Wyllyam Gardynyr.

Tragically, the only mount that Richard was given was the horse over which his now naked and mutilated corpse was then unceremoniously slung – the last English king to die in battle, and the only king to do so on English soil since Harold II, at the Battle of Hastings in 1066.

Tradition tells of Lord Thomas Stanley finding the crown of England, lying in a thorn bush after the battle, and dramatically placing it on Henry Tudor's head. This may only be a legend, but 'Crown Hill' still exists near the site. From this time onwards, Thomas Stanley was known as the 'Kingmaker', and a thorn bush became part of Henry Tudor's heraldic symbolism. Meanwhile, Richard's still naked body was brought to Leicester, where it was publicly displayed to prove his death. A few days later it was buried in an unmarked tomb.

In 1485, upon his accession to the throne, the new King Henry VII rewarded Lord Thomas Stanley by granting him the hereditary Earldom of Derby, a title that the family still hold today.

The many descendants of Thomas and William Stanley have done much to redeem their reputation. Rising to regional supremacy and national significance, over the centuries they have made significant contributions to political, social, and cultural life. They continue to do so, especially in and around Liverpool and Merseyside, where the current Earl, the 19th, is held in great respect and affection.

AD 1588

'THE SPANISH ARE COMING!'

The Scouse Hero of The Spanish Armada

IN THE LATTER decades of the sixteenth century, Catholic King Philip II of Spain (1527–1598) intended to conquer England and remove the Protestant Queen Elizabeth I (1533–1603) from the throne. It is unlikely that he wanted the crown for himself, but intended to place a Catholic in Elizabeth's place – probably Mary Queen of Scots (born 1542). But Elizabeth executed Mary, in 1587, which infuriated Philip and made him more determined than ever to attack England – so he laid his plans.

In 1588, the Spanish King assembled, equipped, and heavily armed a fleet of around 130 mighty warships. On board he had around 17,000 equally well-armed soldiers, ready to invade and attack the English. Also in the fleet were around 200 Catholic priests, ready to do spiritual battle and take command of the souls of the English soldiers and sailors. In July of that year, and under the command of Alonso Perez du Guzman (1550–1615), the son of the 7th Duke of Medina Sidonia, the armada of galleons set sail from Spain.

The King planned for his ships to first make their way to the coast of France, at Dunkirk, where his French allies would allow him to take on board a further 16,000 Spanish troops, under the command of Alessandro Farnese, the Duke of Parma (1545–1592).

The English Navy was expecting the attack, but did not know when it would come. Beacons had been erected around the entire coast of the country, waiting to be lit when the alarm was raised – calling the men and women of England to readiness and resistance against the Spanish invasion. There were a number of such beacons in our area, including one on the summit of Bidston Hill, on the Wirral, and another at the top of Everton Ridge, overlooking the small but important port of Liverpool.

The country waited anxiously, unsure if they would be victorious against the coming attack. Everyone knew just how formidable the Spanish Fleet was going to be, and how vital it would be that England should be victorious against their resolute foe. We had faith in our navy, and in her famous captains, but when would the Spanish attack? We watched from our coastlines, and we anxiously waited.

But then Captain Humphrey Brook from Liverpool, on board his ship *Relief*, which was outward bound from his home and sailing for the Canary Islands, saw the great

Spanish fleet in the distance, sailing north just off the coast of Spain.

Realising what was taking place, he put his helm about and, under full sail, headed back to England – to Plymouth harbour, where the English ships were eagerly waiting to get into battle. As he drew near the harbour he called out, 'Hark! Hark! The Spaniards are sailing towards our shores, send out the warning!'

And the warning did indeed go out; to the English Fleet, at anchor but rigged to sail; to London, to inform the Queen and Parliament; and to the citizens of England. Around the country the alarm was raised and the beacon fires were lit – one after another. A continuous chain of blazing pyres and smoke now began to spread around the highest points of our coastline, reaching skyward and igniting the flames of patriotic fervour in the 'hearts of oak' of England.

And England was indeed ready: our fleet took to the seas and sailed into the English Channel to confront a mighty adversary. But, whilst her soldiers and sailors were fighting for English freedoms, Queen Elizabeth made her way to Tilbury, on the Essex coast, just south of London. Here was stationed an army of a further 2,000 soldiers, standing ready to repel the expected invasion by Spanish troops.

Clad in bright armour with a silver breastplate, and mounted on a white horse, 'Good Queen Bess' positioned herself on high ground so that the men could hear her. Then, in a clear, sharp voice, to her ecstatic soldiers, she declared:

My loving people... Let tyrants fear, I have always so behaved myself, that under God I have placed my chiefest strength and safeguard the loyal hearts and goodwill of my subjects; and, therefore, I am come amongst you, as you see at this time, not for my recreation and disport, but being resolved, in the midst and heat of battle, to live or die amongst you all — to lay down for my God, and for my kingdoms, and for my people, my honour and my blood even in the dust.

I know I have the body of a weak and feeble woman; but I have the heart and stomach of a king — and of a King of England too, and think foul scorn that Parma, or Spain, or any Prince of Europe, should dare to invade the borders of my realm; to which, rather than any dishonour should grow by me, I myself will take up arms — I myself will be your general, judge, and rewarder of every one of your virtues in the field...

Under the command of Captains Hawkins and Frobisher, under Effingham in the *Ark Royal*, and under Drake, in the *Revenge*, the Spanish were not going to have an

The beacon that was lit on Everton Ridge was on the top of a tower that had stood for many centuries before the Spanish set their sights on England. Probably erected around 1230, during the reign of King Henry III (1207-1272), it was 6 yards square and about 25ft high, and was built of plain stone. There was a viewing platform on the roof, with a guardroom below and a kitchen area at ground level.

Towards the end of the eighteenth century, the Beacon was becoming unsafe and, on a very stormy night in 1803, it blew down. St George's church now stands on the site.

Everton Beacon.

easy time. The story goes, of course, that Sir Francis Drake was playing a game of bowls at Plymouth Hoe when the alarm was raised, but insisted on completing his game before taking ship: true English '*sang froid*'!

Thanks to the greater manoeuvrability and firepower of the smaller English vessels – and because of the stout hearts and dauntless courage of the English sailors – the Spanish soon met their match. Thanks too to English fireships sent in against Spanish vessels; and to a stormy English Channel that drove the Spanish fleet north, where it dashed itself against the vicious and unforgiving rocks of the Scottish coast – the rest is history!

But especial thanks are certainly due to Captain Humphrey Brook – the Scouser who first warned his country that the Spanish Armada was on its way and who, quite rightly, was substantially rewarded by Parliament for his speed and honour in defence of his country.

BUBOES, BLOOD, AND BLACK DEATH

Pestilence Stalks the Streets of Liverpool

AT A TIME when vinegar was the only form of disinfectant that people had, the repeated outbreaks of plague that swept Britain from the fourteenth to the seventeenth centuries were of almost biblical proportions. Indeed, their faith was often all that people had to sustain them, as their families, friends, and entire communities were decimated by pestilence.

The first outbreak of the dread disease, which became known as 'The Black Death', began in continental Europe in 1328, and lasted until 1351 – but there were to be further catastrophic outbreaks at various times over the next sixty years. Plague came to England in 1348, and reached Liverpool, and its surrounding villages, between 1359 and 1361. It killed around 500 people and so destroyed half the local population. Even so, Liverpool was luckier than some English villages, which were wiped out entirely. In fact, the country lost between 30 per cent and 40 per cent of its people.

The most vulnerable died first – the very young, the very old, and the poorest. The disease took its more formal name – Bubonic Plague – from the effects on its victims as it destroyed their bodies.

First, swellings – called 'buboes' – appeared in the armpits, legs, neck, or groin: these would be red at first, but would then turn purple, then black: the skin around these swellings would blacken also. Blood-letting was considered to be a legitimate form of treatment at the time but, when the buboes were lanced, the blood that oozed slowly out of the wounds was itself black. It was also rippled with streaks of dark green, was much thicker than normal, and gave off a dreadful stink.

Spread by fleas that were in turn carried on the bodies of rats and mice, it was inevitable that the Black Death would find its way to the steadily growing port of Liverpool, especially as our shipping trade was international. The rodents would scurry down the gangplanks and rope hawsers of the merchant vessels, and make their way amongst the alleys and passages between the houses, going inside them too as they searched for food. Such creatures were a common sight, and they shared living space – and food supplies – with humans. Whilst these rodents may have been regarded as irritating pests, they were a fact of medieval life: it was just that no one realised that they carried pain and death in their matted, filthy fur.

As the rats ran past or brushed against human bodies, the fleas would jump onto new hosts. People would scratch the flea-bites that now afflicted them, and the plague bacteria would find a way into human bloodstreams through the bite-wounds – often driven under the skin by the dirty fingernails of the victims themselves. The lack of any sanitation, and the foul living conditions, only increased the spread of the disease.

From the first flea-bites, a plague victim would soon find buboes emerging on his body. He would rapidly develop a high fever, begin vomiting, and then go into a delirium. Dreadful pains would rack his muscles, and he would lose all sense of time and location. He would see the anguish of his family around him, though, and this would add to his own suffering. Victims would also become very drowsy, but once they slipped into sleep their end was only a very short time away.

The mortality rate in medieval Liverpool may have been high, as it was throughout Britain at that time, but it was especially high amongst the young. Commonplace though infant death was in medieval England, this did not reduce the horror of a mother or father witnessing the misery of their children – especially as the Black Death also caused bleeding in the lungs, so coughing up of black blood was another symptom. The Grim Reaper did not wait long to gather in the victims of his plague; they mostly died within two to four days of those first insect bites. Perhaps, though, that was a blessing, as the symptoms were so dreadful.

However, the fourteenth-century out-breaks of the Black Death were not the last of these that Liverpool was to suffer; it returned in 1558, wiping out a third of the population – around 250 people. All public events – including the markets – had to be cancelled, thus damaging the economy of the town. And this was only a year after the port had fallen prey to another virulent disease – the 'Sweating Sickness', which, between 1557 and 1559, added yet another layer of anguish on the people.

Symptoms of Sweating Sickness began with shivering and feelings of extreme cold, suddenly followed by a high fever and hot sweating all over the body. Accompanied by severe pains in the limbs, shoulders, and neck, this disease killed in a matter of hours. 'Will the Lord not spare our tormented souls?' was the cry that went up. And, for a few years, it seemed as though that prayer had been answered; but only until 1610, when the Black Death struck again. And then it came again, in 1648, and again, in 1651, and once more, in 1656.

There was absolutely no understanding of how the plague was caused or carried, and only rudimentary knowledge of medicine. No cure was known, so all that could be done was to try to relieve the symptoms.

A mixture of comfrey and liquorice was given to people to drink, in the hope this would stop them coughing up blood.

Sweating Sickness seemed to be most virulent amongst the higher classes of English society. Some historians believe that it may have been Sweating Sickness that so tragically afflicted the family of King Henry VIII, killing his older brother, Prince Arthur. Anne Boleyn may also have suffered from it, and, whilst she survived (at least, until Henry decapitated her), the disease killed many members of the Royal Court.

Wormwood and mint were used to try and halt vomiting; and sage and bay leaves, combined with lavender and rose petals, were applied in an attempt to relieve headaches. To try to deal with the buboes, a paste of onion and garlic mixed with butter was smeared over the body: even dried frogs and toads were used as treatments – but nothing worked.

All that could be done was to collect up the bodies – men, women, and children – and bury them in large pits. There were too many to go in the churchyards, which very soon filled up with ravaged corpses.

Such a pit was dug near Liverpool's parish church, at Walton-On-The-Hill, with many others in places away from centres of population. The locations of these lonely final resting places have often been lost in time, only to be rediscovered by chance. In the modern Liverpool suburb of Old Swan, once an isolated hill-top well outside the ancient town, such grisly remnants of the Black Death were found in 1973.

As foundations were being dug for St Oswald's Primary Schools some human remains were unearthed. Work had to be halted for eighteen months whilst further excavations were carried out. To everyone's surprise, however, these revealed more than 3,500 coffins and skeletons – some piled sixteen deep. Clearly these were plague victims – perhaps from the fourteenth century, when the Black Death first came to Liverpool and all of its surrounding villages.

This was a stark reminder of just how close we can still be to the tragedies of our past.

Horrors of the plague!
Piles of naked corpses being carted away,
whilst yet more dead lie waiting to be collected.

AD 1644

THE SIEGE AND MASSACRE OF LIVERPOOL

A Bloodbath In The Seven Streets

FROM THE BEGINNING of the seventeenth century, Liverpool had begun to develop into an important port and trading centre. Despite the repeated outbreaks of plague, the people of the town were determined to overcome adversity, and continued to invest in the future of their community. More and more people were coming here, to settle in what was a place of increasing opportunity.

But then a calamity fell upon the people of England: Civil War broke out between Parliament and King Charles I (1600–1649), lasting from 1642 to 1651. Land, villages, and towns changed hands – sometimes more than once – throughout this brutal conflict. And Liverpool was a prize that both sides of the conflict wanted: its strategic location, resources, and considerable fortifications made it a valuable site.

When King John had established the town, in 1207, he had instructed that seven streets be laid out in an 'H' formation, and these were still the core of the town. Dominating the small community was a formidable castle, with a deep moat and bastions, built in the early years of the thirteenth century. This stood on high land in the centre of the town, and was under the hereditary constableship of the aristo-cratic Molyneux family. They were staunch Royalists, whilst the town's sympathies were mostly with the Parliamentarians.

Also supporters of the King, though bitter rivals of the Molyneuxs, were the Stanley family; direct descendants of Sir Thomas Stanley, and so hereditary Earls of Derby. Their base was on the riverfront, at the bottom of Water Street, in the intimidating Tower of Liverpool. This was a large fortified mansion house – with cellars, dungeons, towers, and turrets – and it was as strategic to the port, its pool, and the river, as was the castle.

In 1632, the Roman Catholic Molyneux family (later the Earls of Sefton) had acquired the Manorial rights to the town, giving them great dominance over civic affairs. And so, when the Civil War broke out, and with the population of Liverpool reduced to around 1,000 people by repeated outbreaks of plague, they encouraged the Royalists to take control of the town and the castle, which they duly did.

Then, in April 1643, the town was recaptured by the Parliamentarians – following a brief siege. However, some Royalist sympathisers escaped the town and made their way to other communities outside the boundaries; many going to the Royalist stronghold at the nearby village of Everton, high above the town on Everton Ridge. Other supporters of the King – including the Molyneuxs – stayed within the town and kept quiet about their allegiances, but they were simply biding their time.

The vast majority of the town's population at this time were still for the civil freedoms offered by the opponents of the monarch – a precursor perhaps to the militancy of later generations of Scousers! However, they knew only too well that a Royalist attempt to re-take the town was inevitable. Soon, King Charles I ordered his twenty-four-year-old nephew, Prince Rupert of the Rhine (1619–1682), to recapture Liverpool. Always a dashing and elegant figure, and invariably accompanied by his pet dog and monkey, Rupert was nevertheless a ruthless soldier who had commanded his first cavalry regiment at the age of only fourteen.

Arriving on the evening of the 1 June 1644, the German Prince set up his headquarters in the Royalist redoubt of

Prince Rupert, who savagely attacked Liverpool.

Everton, which afforded outstanding overviews of the town, and he commandeered a spacious cottage in the village, standing in a road known as Browside. From this time, until its eighteenth-century demolition, this would be known as 'Prince Rupert's Cottage'.

With him, Rupert had brought an army of 10,000 soldiers to attack the town, and his men camped – with their horses, munitions, and supplies, on land now to the right of Heyworth Street, opposite Everton Ridge. The Prince had already savagely attacked another northern town, Bolton, and this news had reached Liverpool as he marched towards it. This struck terror in the people, so the decision was taken to evacuate the women and children to the safety of Wallasey, Seacombe, and Storeton, across the Mersey on the Wirral.

In the meantime, the town's defenders, now under the command of its Parliamentarian Governor, Colonel Moore, had surrounded Liverpool with high, defensive mud embankments, and wooden palisades. In front of the wall was a ditch, 12 yards wide and 3 deep. Also, the Liverpudlians mounted a number of cannon on the castle towers and battlements. At the entrance to the Pool Harbour – where the Liverpool ONE retail complex now stands – they had established a powerful battery of mortars.

The men and youths who remained in the town, numbering around 450, were fully armed with muskets and pikes; they were ready to die in defence of their homes. But all of this was known to Prince Rupert, because the Molyneuxs acted as a 'fifth column' within the town, and were smuggling messages out to him. Consequently, the rash young man believed that taking Liverpool would be a simple matter. Indeed, he declared that the town was, 'nought but a crow's nest that a parcel of boys could take'.

Rupert's cannon were arrayed from where the Wellington Column now dominates William Brown Street, to a point now occupied by the Adelphi Hotel. On 6 June, and firing above the town's outlying mills, farmsteads, and cottages, and over the broad creek that fed the Pool, the German Prince besieged Liverpool.

Although subjecting the people to a constant barrage of artillery, the arrogant aristocrat was soon to discover, to his cost, that the resistance mounted by the townspeople was considerable and determined. After a continuous cannonade against the town, Rupert had been forced to use over 100 barrels of powder in numerous bombardments, and had lost 1,500 of his men in the returned fire from the embattled Liverpudlians. The town had only lost about forty-five men in these assaults, so Rupert had vastly underestimated his adversaries.

However, this only stiffened the Prince's resolve and, on the 11 June 1644, he ordered a secret, night-time attack; again secretly aided by the Royalist sympathisers, led by Caryll Molyneux. In the dead of night, these traitors to their own townsfolk breached the defensive walls from within, in the section across Old Hall Street, and Rupert's troops now poured into Liverpool. Their assault was a swift and exceptionally brutal massacre, as the Prince's men put everyone they encountered to the sword.

The town of Liverpool, seen from the waterfront, during the time of the Civil War.

After Prince Rupert had been ordered to leave Liverpool, he decided that the loot of the town would be an encumbrance. So he instructed that, for safekeeping, the treasure should be buried in a tunnel that still runs from under the site of his cottage, beneath Netherfield Road, down to the dock road at the Strand. The gold and treasure was never heard of again, and it is believed to still lie there, hidden beneath modern Liverpool. Perhaps all that is needed now is a latter-day Scouse 'Indiana Jones' to rediscover it!

During the siege and the subsequent sacking of Liverpool, over 360 defenders lost their lives, and the town records relate that of these were 'some that had never borne arms... yea, even one poor blind man'. Caryll Molyneux had personally slaughtered a number of the townsmen, and the memory of this cruelty, and of his treachery, lived long in the hearts of Liverpool's people, colouring their views of the Molyneux family for generations.

Once the battle was over and all resistance had been quashed, Rupert ordered the complete sacking and firing of the town, which was plundered of all its money, gold, and treasures, and was left in smoking ruins. Liverpool Castle was one of the few buildings that survived the assault largely intact, and Rupert stayed there for nine nights. Leaving a garrison behind, he then moved on to York, on the orders of the King.

It then took the surviving men of Liverpool, and the returning women and children, six months to finish burying their dead.

However, things were not going well for the armies of the monarch and, on 20 August 1644, the Royalists were defeated at nearby Ormskirk, retreating in disarray to Liverpool, where they joined the existing Royalist occupiers. But the Parliamentarians were in hot pursuit, and now it was they who laid siege to the poor, beleaguered town.

The Royalists had all now withdrawn to the relative protection of the castle, but the old bastion became the main target of a relentless Roundhead bombardment and was severely damaged. Soon, the exhausted garrison could take no more, and they mutinied against their officers – giving up the town to the now victorious Parliamentarians.

Fortunately for the defeated soldiers, the attacking troops were more humane in their victory than the Royalists had been in theirs, and the lives of the captured officers were spared. They were allowed to retreat in safety to Ireland. Lord Derby was also captured by Roundhead soldiers, and we shall learn of his fate in a later chapter of this bloody history of Liverpool and its people.

In the wake of the conflict, the people of Liverpool held the Molyneux family directly responsible for their decimated population and devastated homes and property. So, these descendants of the Norman invaders quietly withdrew to their Croxteth estates. But this was only for a time because, in the succeeding centuries, and like the Stanley family, they were to once again become significant in the pages of Liverpool's, and Britain's, history.

AD 1644

A COOL HEAD AND A LOST ONE

Cromwell's Revenge on a Lord of Liverpool

THROUGHOUT MOST OF its history, Liverpool had two aristocratic Lords; the Earls of Sefton (descended from the Molyneux family), and the Earls of Derby (descended from the Stanley family). After the Civil War, both families lost their estates, but regained them at the restoration of the monarchy in 1660. However, James Stanley, the 7th Earl of Derby, was to lose more than his lands.

Unlike the Molyneuxs, the Stanley family had remained popular in Liverpool – and throughout the north of England – despite their support of King Charles I (1600–1649). This was because they had always been honourable and loyal to the town, particularly James Stanley. Nevertheless, he fought boldly and bravely for the cause in which he believed.

James Stanley had been born, in 1607, at the family seat of Knowsley, just to the south-east of Liverpool. In July 1626, he had married Charlotte de la Tremouille (1599–1664), a woman of formidable personality and remarkable strength of character. Both of these qualities would eventually be put to the test, but, for a few years at least, they were able to settle into married life. Theirs was a love-match, and they raised a family of six children at their other estate, Lathom House, near Ormskirk. But, in 1642, the English Civil War began.

James immediately declared for the King, and began to recruit men and raise arms for the Royalists. He also commandeered the stores of weapons and gunpowder in Lancaster and Liverpool Castles. On 28 September of that year his father died, and James Stanley became the Earl of Derby and Charlotte his Countess. He was also the leading Royalist in the north-west of England.

In 1643, at the King's command, James – who had also inherited the title of Lord of the Isle of Man – went to that island to subdue a rebellion by the Manx people, and 'to keep the Isle of Man for His Majesty's service, against all force whatever'.

After succeeding in this mission, the Earl returned to the north of England to join the King's campaign there, leaving his wife, the redoubtable Charlotte, in charge of the house and estates at Lathom. This was to become the last remaining Royalist stronghold in Lancashire, in the face of advancing Parliamentary forces under the command of Sir Thomas Fairfax (1612–1671).

Lathom House, seat of the Stanleys.

Fairfax saw Stanley's absence as an opportunity to capture a major prize in the mansion and lands at Lathom and, after all, they were now only being held by a woman! But Fairfax was to meet his match.

In February 1644, marching his troops up to the gates of the house, Fairfax demanded that, 'The Lady Charlotte shall straightway acknowledge the authority of the parliament and surrender house and lands'. Although Lady Derby had a large garrison of troops at her command, she did not want to engage in battle, knowing that the house and estates would be destroyed in the conflict. Instead, she sent back the following message: 'To surrender would dishonour my husband, which I shall not do, and, whilst I shall not attack my enemies, I shall surely defend his lands and properties.'

Her cool head and firm resolve stalled Fairfax and, because she had said she would not attack him, and unsure of how strong her forces actually were, the general held off his own attack. Even so, he sent Charlotte another demand for her surren-der. She replied that she would 'hang any further messengers from the gates of my tower'!

So Fairfax put Lathom House, with Lady Charlotte and her family, under siege; but she still refused to surrender.

Then, on the night of 27 May 1644, Prince Rupert of the Rhine approached Lathom with thousands of cavalry and infantry, driving off Fairfax and his Parliamentarians. The Prince then urged Lady Charlotte to go to the Isle of Man, with her family and household. Not willingly, but eventually obeying the Prince's orders, she landed on the island on 30 July; she left her house and lands intact and protected because of her coolness and courage.

Soon to be joined by her husband on the Isle of Man, for a number of years the Earl and Countess lived in exile, in their family stronghold at Castle Rushen.

In due course, King Charles I lost the Civil War, and was captured, tried, and then executed, in 1649. Parliament had commandeered all of the Stanley holdings in England by this time, but now they offered the Earl half his estates in exchange for the surrender of the Isle of Man. Following his wife's noble example, he responded by saying, 'I scorn your proffers, disdain your favour and abhor your treason, and am so far from delivering up this Island to your advantage, that I will keep it to the utmost of my power and your destruction'.

But then, in 1650, the 'King in waiting', Charles II (1630–1685), landed in Scotland to reclaim the throne, where he was immediately recognised as the true King. In 1651, he then began to march southwards, through north-west England, with an army of 16,000 men, determined to complete his mission.

On 15 August 1651, and with the passionate endorsement of his Countess, the Earl left the Isle of Man, landing in England to support Charles, with about 250 foot soldiers and about 100 cavalry. After many battles and skirmishes with Cromwell's troops, and always being relentlessly pursued by them, James was exhausted.

Charles had temporarily given up his attempt to regain the crown, and had escaped abroad. This so dispirited Lord Derby that, in September 1651, he finally surrendered to Parliamentary forces.

Lord Derby was taken to Chester Castle to await a court martial, on charges of 'assisting the declared traitor Charles Stuart to invade England'. The verdict of the court martial was inevitable, as the Government was determined to make an example of the Earl. Sentence of death was pronounced on 1 October 1651, and this would be carried out in the marketplace at Bolton.

James wrote to his beloved wife, saying, 'whatsoever comes on me, I have peace in my own breast, and no discomfort at all but the sense of your grief, and that of my poor children and friends.'

The Reverend Humphrey Baggarley accompanied the Earl on his journey from Chester to Bolton, and wrote a detailed account of the events:

...on Wednesday the 15th October 1651, the Earl of Derby came to Bolton... The people everywhere praying and weeping as he went, even from the castle of Chester, his prison, to his scaffold at Bolton... saying that since the War began they had suffered many and great losses; but never so great as this. This was the greatest that ever befell them; that the Earl of Derby, their Lord and Patriot, should lose his life there, and in such a barbarous manner.

At his going towards the scaffold, the people cried and prayed... he laid his hands upon the ladder, saying, 'I am not afraid to go up here, though to my death.'

...His Lordship walking the scaffold, called for his Executioner to come to him, and asked to feel the axe, saying, 'Come friend, give it into my hands, I'll neither hurt thee or it; and it cannot hurt me, for I am not afraid of it.' So kissing it, gave it to him again, and asked to feel the block...

Then putting his hand into his pocket, he gave the Headsman two pieces of gold, saying, 'This is all I have, take it, and do thy work well, and when I am upon the

Oliver Cromwell, whose troops pursued Lord Derby.

Proportionally, more people died in the English Civil War than in any other war fought by Britain – including those of the twentieth century. In the seven years that the Civil War lasted, an estimated one in ten British people were killed – the country was, quite literally, decimated. 85,000 people died on the battlefields, and another 100,000 of their wounds. In percentage of population terms, this was three times more than those killed in the First World War, and five times more than those killed in the Second World War.

block and lifting up my hands, then do your business ..."

Then taking off his doublet, he asked how he should lie, saying, 'I never saw anyone's head cut off, but I'll try how it fits.'

So laying himself down and stretching himself upon the block and, after another prayer to God to look after his wife and children, he stretched out his arms, and said, loudly, 'Blessed be God's holy name for ever and ever. Amen. Let the whole earth be filled with His glory.'

And then lifting up his hands the Executioner did his work... After which nothing was heard in the town but sighs, sobs, and prayers.

On the following Friday, a sad procession took Earl James's body through Lancashire, from Bolton to Ormskirk, where he was laid to rest in the Derby Chapel in the parish church. People along the route displayed their grief, because, for most Lancastrians, his beheading was regarded as an unnecessary and undeserved death.

Lord Derby had fought bravely, and with honour, for a cause in which he fervently believed was the best for his country and its people. He lost his head for his convictions, and his family lost their estates and authority – for a few years, at least.

His wife, the brave, redoubtable Lady Charlotte, had kept her wits – and her head – at great personal risk. But she too kept her honour, and her courage saved her own life and those of her children; including her son Charles, who now became the 8th Earl of Derby.

AD 1716

HOW THE GALLOWS MILL TAVERN GOT ITS NAME

A Spectacle of Horror

FOR MANY YEARS the only buildings in London Road were some windmills and an isolated inn, known as the 'Gallows Mill Tavern'. Standing close to the road's junction with what is now Stafford Street, this was the site of a special gallows and scaffold.

This had been built to perform a particularly gruesome service, following the Jacobite rebellions in the middle years of the eighteenth century. But these major military uprisings had their roots in the Civil War, and the animosity between Catholic and Protestant.

In 1685, King Charles II died, but not before converting to Catholicism on his deathbed. Not having a legitimate heir, although he had plenty of children who were not, the throne was inherited by his brother, who became King James II (1633–1701).

In 1669, James too had converted to Catholicism, but this did not prevent his succession, although some in the country were concerned by his faith, and by his attempts to install fellow Catholics in influential positions. One such rebel was Charles II's illegitimate son, the Duke of Monmouth (1649–1685), who raised an

London Road, where the Gallows Mill once stood.

On 15 July 1685, the Duke of Monmouth was to be beheaded on Tower Hill in London, by the notorious executioner Jack Ketch. But Ketch botched the job. He took between five and eight attempts to complete the decapitation, with the tragic Duke screaming for mercy all the while.

An apocryphal tale went the rounds that, after the execution, it was realised that no portrait of the Duke had ever been painted, so his head was sewn back on again to allow an artist to do so.

army and marched from Scotland against the King. This was speedily quashed, and Monmouth was executed.

Then, in 1688, James had a son, James Francis Edward (died 1766), which convinced other Protestant nobles that a Catholic succession was about to be imposed on them. They invited the Protestant Prince, William of Orange (1650–1702), from the Netherlands, to take the throne. In what became known as 'The Glorious Revolution', William landed with an army in Devon, whilst the King had assembled a force of troops to defend his crown. However, James's army and navy deserted him, forcing him to flee abroad. William of Orange, with his wife, Mary (1662–1694), was crowned joint monarchs that same year.

They were succeeded by the Protestant Kings George I (1660–1727), in 1714, and then by George II (1683–1760), but both monarchs had to deal with rebellions from members of the exiled Stuart dynasty, each determined to reclaim the English throne and rule as Catholics.

The most significant of these uprisings were known as 'The Jacobite Rebellions' – taking their name from 'Jacobus', the Latin form of James. The 'First Jacobite Rebellion' took place in 1715, so became known as 'The Fifteen'. This was led by James Francis Edward (1688–1766), who later became known as 'The Old Pretender'.

Coming to Scotland from his place of exile in France, James soon found his rebellion collapsing, almost as soon as it had started – despite some ferocious fighting between rebel and Government troops. The Jacobites suffered major defeats at the battles of Preston and Sheriffmuir, and many rebels were slaughtered. James abandoned his lost cause, leaving England for France again, never to return. A number of rebels were executed, others were deported, peerages were forfeited, and Scottish clans were disarmed.

The 'Second Jacobite Rebellion' took place in 1745, so became known as 'The Forty-Five'. This was led by the son of the Old Pretender, Charles Edward Stuart (the Young Pretender, 1720–1788): better known to history as 'Bonnie Prince Charlie'. The twenty-five-year-old was to have much greater success in his uprising than his father had experienced – up to a point!

Sailing to Scotland from France – also his place of exile – Charles raised the Jacobite standard at Glenfinnan in the Scottish Highlands, where he was supported by a gathering of Highland clansmen. They first marched towards Edinburgh, where they were victorious at the Battle of Prestonpans. Confident of further victories, they crossed the border into England.

Making their way to Carlisle, the Jacobites then continued deeper into the north-west, heading towards Liverpool.

The Gallows Mill Tavern, which was built close to the site of the execution scaffold.

Panic spread before them, except in the town, which was staunchly Georgian: the people here were ready to repel the rebels and defend themselves. A volunteer force of over 2,000 men mustered from the town; it was funded by the Liverpool Corporation and public subscription. These were called the 'Liverpool Blues'.

Despite the town's fears, however, Bonnie Prince Charlie carefully avoided Liverpool, but he did get as far as Derby. The 'Blues' fought victoriously on the side of the King against the Young Pretender, and he was driven all the way back to Scotland again, retreating to Inverness. In acknowledgment of their loyalty and courage, the Liverpool troops received the honour of a Royal Inspection by the King's brother, the Duke of Cumberland. To acknowledge and reciprocate this honour, the town laid out new streets and named them after the Duke – Hanover, Duke, and Cumberland Streets, each of which still exists.

It was near Inverness that the final battle of the Jacobite Rebellion was fought, and it was also the last battle ever fought on British soil, at the moor known as Culloden. Bonnie Prince Charlie led an army made up of a number of Scottish clans, which was attacked by the Duke of Cumberland, lead-ing the King's troops. The Duke won the battle but offered little mercy to the rebels – becoming known ever afterwards as 'The Butcher of Culloden'. The Young Pretender had fled the battlefield, and wandered around the Highlands of Scotland during the summer of 1746. He soon returned to France, and permanent exile, where he died.

Punishment for captured Jacobites, following both rebellions, was swift, merciless, and brutal. Indeed, after the first Jacobite Rebellion had been put down, prisoners awaiting trial were held in the ancient gaols of Lancaster, Preston, Chester, and in the unwholesome dungeons of the Tower of Liverpool.

Between the 20 January and the 9 February 1716, a specially convened court was held in Liverpool, to try seventy-four Jacobites for high treason: sixty of them were found guilty. Of those men who had admitted their offence, many avoided the death penalty. Some were transported, whilst others were imprisoned. But their prison conditions were so harsh that many of them died anyway, of disease or malnutrition. But thirty-four men were sentenced to be executed, in various towns around the north-west, as an example and a deterrent.

And what a grisly end it was to be too: the traitors' death by 'Hanging, Drawing, and Quartering'.

This sadistic form of execution was invented, in 1241, specifically to punish a man called William Maurice who had been convicted of piracy. In 1283, Dafydd ap Gruffydd, the last Welsh Prince of Wales (born *c.* 1235) also died this way, as did William Wallace (*c.* 1270–1305), better known as 'Braveheart', at Smithfield in London. Guy Fawkes and his fellow 'Gunpowder Plot' conspirators had also been victims of this terrible punishment in 1606, but now it was the turn of the Jacobite rebels.

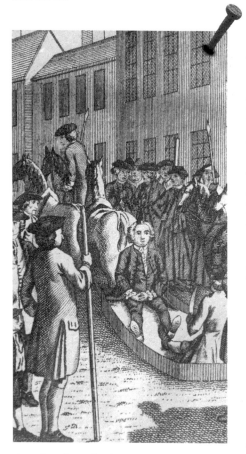

A Jacobite dragged to his awful death. The man sitting on the sledge with him is the executioner: he is waving the knife with which he will cut out the prisoner's entrails.

On 15 February 1716, four terrified prisoners, whom records list as 'a Mr Burnett, Alexander Drummond, George Collingwood, and John Hunter', were dragged from the dungeons of the Tower of Liverpool, where they had been held. They were tied to a type of sledge, and horses pulled this through the streets of the town, to its outskirts. Here, near three windmills, a specially-constructed scaffold-platform, with a gallows, had been erected.

Then, in front of a very large crowd, the condemned men faced their executioners – this complex penalty required a number of such professionals to carry it out, who were paid £10 and 3 shillings each for their work. With the last of the prisoners forced to witness the other three die before him, in turn, the gruesome process began.

First, the victim was stripped naked, and hanged by the neck from the gallows, slowly strangling. Then, and just before death, he was taken down, still living, stretched spread-eagled on the scaffold platform, and tied down by his wrists and ankles. His genitals were then hacked off, and burned in a fire in front of his eyes. Next, his belly was slit open and his intestines were slowly pulled out of him, or 'drawn'. These too were then burned before his eyes.

Only when this process was complete would the screaming man, awash with his own blood, be put out of his anguish by having his head slowly sawn off. His mutilated body was then cut into four quarters, each one to be displayed on a pike, in a different town in the region; again, as an example and deterrent.

Women traitors were much more fortunate though – to preserve public decency they were only slowly roasted alive as they burned at the stake!

That is how the tavern – now long-since vanished – got its name: Gallows Mill.

AD 1745

THE CASTLE AND THE TOWER

Dungeons, Turrets, Towers and Torment

IN SOME OF the stories I have already told about the grislier sides of Liverpool's history, I have made mention of the town's two ancient fortifications: Liverpool Castle and the Tower of Liverpool. Now it is time for me to tell the tale of these buildings themselves.

In Derby Square, where Lord Street, Castle Street, and James Street meet, once stood Liverpool Castle. The construction of the town's great stronghold had begun before the death of King John, in 1216. The work was completed sometime between 1232 and 1237, by the then Lord of the Manor and Sheriff of Lancaster, William de Ferrers – it was to stand for around 500 years.

The castle was an impressive stone structure, erected on the highest point between the River Mersey and the original tidal 'Pool' of Liverpool. This afforded excellent views, not just of the surrounding land but also of the river, and so it was in a particularly strategic position. The castle was built out of massive sandstone blocks, and was surrounded by a moat, mostly hewn out of the solid rock.

The building was designed to be self-sufficient in times of siege; consequently, the castle had its own bake-house, brew-house, and well. There was also an apple orchard on the west side of the castle, overlooking the river, and a stone-built dovecot to the south.

The de Ferrers family, their servants, and their soldiers occupied the castle until 1266, when it was taken over by other nobles. By 1347, the castle's facilities had developed, and there were now a large hall, and a chapel in the main courtyard. The hall was big enough to be a dining space for all the occupants, and this also provided full stabling for the horses and other livestock. People and animals tended to occupy the same space in those days – imagine the smell!

The fortress was rectangular in design, with tall, broad, circular towers at three of its corners, and a large gatehouse, barbican, and portcullis at its fourth. Another tower was added in 1441. The entrance was also guarded by a drawbridge and portcullis, on a causeway across the broad, deep moat. The towers and barbican were connected by high, curtain walls topped by battlements, and these strong defences enclosed a broad courtyard.

Liverpool Castle also had deep cellars and, in all likelihood, dark, damp dungeons. The purpose of a dungeon was

*The dreadful and formidable Tower of Liverpool, and
a postcard view of Castle Street. The castle once stood
at the point where Lord Street and Castle Street meet
James Street.*

for temporarily holding prisoners or, in extreme cases, for torturing them – English history is awash with tales of the rack, the wheel, the 'Scavenger's Daughter', the boots, and the thumbscrews. Whilst there is no evidence that Liverpool Castle was ever used for such purposes, it is not certain that it wasn't.

In the early 1980s, as Derby Square was being excavated for new Law Courts, the dried and perfectly preserved corpse of a Roundhead soldier was found, complete with uniform, in what appears to have been a deep cell or dungeon. Had he been locked up and left to starve to death? We are unlikely ever to know.

For centuries the castle had dominated the small town of Liverpool; its great towers and imposing gateway reminding the townspeople of where exactly lay the true power in the land. It was certainly not with them, but in the hands of the aristocracy – mostly descendants of the Norman invaders of 1066.

It took the Civil War to put an end to the castle, which was severely damaged in the final siege on the town, but it was not completely cleared away until 1726. Nothing now remains, above ground, to say that a castle ever stood there, save a small plaque noting the fact, mounted on the side of Queen Victoria's memorial. The Old Queen has been gazing sternly down Lord Street – named after Lord Molyneux – since 1902.

But the tale of the Tower of Liverpool is much darker.

On the Strand – once literally a strand of sand and shingle – and at the bottom of Water Street – in medieval times the gateway to the river – gleams Tower Buildings, looking rather like an ornate wedding cake. It faces the Royal Liver Buildings across the main road, and both buildings were designed by the same architect, Walter Aubrey Thomas (1859–1934). Tower Buildings was completed in 1908, replacing a block of offices built in 1846, this itself replacing old warehouses, constructed in 1819.

But the Tower of Liverpool, which had originally stood on this site, was, for 600 years, the terror of the town.

From around 1250, and facing directly onto the frequently turbulent waters of the River Mersey, stood a large mansion house built of great red sandstone blocks. No one knows who its builder or first owner was but, by the late 1400s, it had passed into the ownership of the Stanley family, the Earls of Derby.

Before this, however, in 1406, Sir John Stanley (c. 1350–1414) had been granted the Lordship of the Isle of Man by King Henry IV (1399–1413). To match his new status, Sir John realised he needed to demonstrate his power and authority, not just to the people but to his great rivals the Molyneux family who, by this time, had

---

In Derby Square, in the cellar under Castle Moat House, a large section of the old castle moat survives. In the middle of what is now a surfaced and brick-lined cellar stand the massive columns that support the current building. In the middle of the floor, and under a wooden trapdoor, is a short access shaft to a very ancient tunnel. This once led from the moat to the bottom of James Street, which was the original shoreline of the river. These are the only remnants now of the once formidable Liverpool Castle.

Queen Victoria's Memorial just after it was built. A tiny plaque is all that remains to suggest a castle ever stood upon this site.

become established in Liverpool Castle, only a few hundred yards away on top of the hill.

He transformed the mansion into a fortified military stronghold, large enough to garrison with his own troops. He added battlements, strong walls, turrets, a fortified gateway, two large central courtyards, and deep dungeons and cellars: he named this new fortress 'The Tower'. For 250 years this was the Stanley family headquarters in Liverpool, and the base from which they governed their 'Kingdom of Man', in the Irish Sea.

Soon after the Civil War the Stanley family sold the Tower and, by 1737, Liverpool Corporation was using the building. This is when the imposing structure entered the second phase of its gruesome life.

By 1745, the upper floors were being used as assembly rooms for dancing, cards, and other entertainments: all this whilst the cellars and dungeons became the town gaol. Conditions were foul beyond belief for the unfortunate people who found themselves incarcerated there. Men, women, boys, and girls were all herded together, with no discrimination, and in often violent, gross, and indecent circumstances. Strong prisoners bullied the weak, and a thriving extortion racket was a principal feature of Tower life, which was harsh and brutal.

There were seven cells, each around 6ft square and all well below ground level. In each of these at least three prisoners could be confined. The only light and air coming into them entered through a small aperture above each cell door. There was no water supply to them, or sanitation, so sickness and death were the prisoners' close companions.

The filth that accumulated could often be ankle-deep, and would only be removed (by the prisoners under close guard) when the happy revellers in the rooms upstairs could no longer stand the stench! This was especially bad in hot weather. Even then, it would only be taken into the centre of one of the two courtyards, where it was piled up in a huge midden that was only emptied once a month. These sewage-covered yards were also the only places where the prisoners could get any exercise.

Food was of appalling quality and far from regularly available, which meant that starving prisoners were often reduced to catching and eating rats and mice to survive.

There was a larger cell in the Tower, on the ground floor. This was big enough to accommodate ten to twelve people, but at one point it was home to over forty. This did have a high window, which faced out onto the street. And so, dependent on the charity of the public, the prisoners lowered gloves or bags, tied to strings suspended from sticks, out into the street, hoping that kindly passers-by would drop in coins or food. Sadly, it was a favourite sport of the local boys to deposit excrement, stones, mud, or other waste and litter into the begging-bags – life was callous in those distant days.

The great prison reformer, John Howard (1726–1790), came to Liverpool in the years 1774 and 1778, to inspect the town's treatment of its prisoners. His report on the dreadful conditions in the dungeons and cells of the Tower of Liverpool scandalised the townspeople. Pressure was brought to bear on the Corporation, and a new, modern Borough Gaol was erected on a new street, named Great Howard Street in tribute to the reformer.

But not before the old prison became the backdrop for public executions, whilst other punishments took place inside. These included flogging, branding, and a particularly nasty form of penalty, known as 'pressing'. Until the time of Queen Anne, it was usual for every jail to have a 'pressing yard', and victims would first be stripped naked and then tied to the stone floor by their wrists and ankles. A flat board would then be laid on their chests, on which an increasing number and weight of heavy stones would be placed. Both men and women could suffer in this way – being crushed to death was a slow and ghastly way to die.

The dreadful Tower of Liverpool was closed in 1811, and demolished soon afterwards.

AD 1778

PILLAGING THE HIGH SEAS

Shot, Shell and Piratical Plunder

DURING THE LATE sixteenth century, and throughout the seventeenth century in particular, pirate activity off the Mersey coast was a major problem for Liverpool vessels. In 1659 alone, around a dozen merchant ships from Liverpool and Chester were captured, with great loss of life and cargo. But on the High Seas and around Britain's coastal waters, this 'scourge of the High Seas and of honest seafarers' was not what it seemed. In fact, not all pirates flew the flag of the 'Skull and Crossbones'. A great number flew the flags of their own countries, including England, and many of these were from Liverpool. They were the 'privateers' – the 'legalised pirates'.

A privateer was the name given to a vessel belonging to a private individual or company who had been granted a special licence, known as a 'Letter of Marque'. These were issued by the Admiralty, in the name of the monarch, to the ship's captain. He could then put to sea and hunt down merchant vessels belonging to whichever country England happened to be at war with at the time: over the centuries, this provided a wide range of opportunity.

This permission to plunder and loot had been around for some time and, during the reign of 'Good Queen Bess', Sir Francis Drake (*c*. 1540- *c*. 1596) was one of this country's most famous and successful privateer captains. In 1563, Sir Thomas Stanley of Hooton, on the Wirral, the son of the Earl of Derby, fitted out a ship as a privateer. He armed his vessel with cannon and his men with pistols and swords, and succeeded in capturing and plundering a foreign merchantman. He brought the ship, with its rich cargo and gold, back to Liverpool, 'amidst great rejoicing from the townsfolk'.

This was because the town took its slice of the profits from such a prize too. Each crew member would get his percentage, as would the captain. The owner would take the lion's share, but the levy from the Corporation would pay for many civic improvements and building projects – including, in 1754, the construction of a new Town Hall. Steadily, the number of privateers operating out of the port began to increase.

But then the town paid a huge sum of money to architect Thomas Steers (*c*. 1670–1750), to enclose and reclaim the Pool of Liverpool, and to create the world's first commercial wet dock. Opening in 1715, this began the town's dramatic rise to become a hub of international com-

Town Hall and Mansion House, Liverpool, built with the Corporation levy on the spoils of the privateers.

merce, and more and more docks, wharves, quays, and warehouses began to be built. As the volume of shipping now increased dramatically, in and out of the town, a boomtime began for Liverpool privateers.

Such sea-borne enterprises could be largely risk-free, because privateers would be heavily armed whilst merchant ships were seldom so equipped. This meant that you could avoid all risk to your own safety, by targeting, shooting at, disabling, and disarming your opponent's vessel from a distance, thus forcing their surrender without any close-quarter cutlass-work at all.

This new breed of merchant adventurer would be more of a 'spectator-pirate' than a hands-on cut-throat. No one-legged, Devonshire-accented sea-cooks here; and no parrots on shoulders either, screeching 'Pieces of Eight'!.

Whilst the crew of a privateer might indeed be rough, tough, hard-living and even harder-drinking sea-dogs, their captains, and certainly their owners – who often sailed with them – were more likely to be merchants and traders. They would have been used to the salons and gentlemen's clubs of Liverpool rather than 'a life on the ocean wave'.

But privateer captains left little to chance. During the mid-eighteenth century there were a number of such vessels licensed to operate from Liverpool: ships included the *Thurloe*, with 100 men and twelve cannon, and the *Terrible* and the *Old Noll*, each with 180 men and twenty-two cannon. Manned by skilled gunners, they wreaked havoc on French and Prussian merchant ships, killing many sailors and claiming vast quantities of booty.

This was also the time of the wars with America and, by 1779, Liverpool was home to 120 privateer vessels; they were owned by entrepreneurs and investors for whom the financial returns could be vast. But, by this time, foreign merchant ships were being protected by warships from their own countries – often now much

Fortunatus Wright (1712-1757) was born in Wallasey, and became the 'celebrity privateer' of his day. He was originally a brewer, but decided that life at sea as a trader would be more profitable and definitely exciting.

In 1744, his ship, *Swallow*, was captured by a French privateer. Fortunatus now decided to become a privateer himself, so that he could take his revenge. In a new ship, *Fame*, he captured sixteen French merchantmen and claimed them as prizes, with a value of £400,000 pounds – at eighteenth-century rates!

Fortunatus's luck ran out on 16 March 1757, when his ship foundered in a storm of the coast of Tuscany, and was lost with all hands.

more heavily-armed than the privateers. But what did it matter if a Liverpool merchant lost one or two vessels, and their crews? It only took one successful venture to make a fortune: life was cheap and profit was all.

Such an opportunist was Peter Baker – although his success was more by luck than design.

Originally a joiner by trade, Baker set up a ship-building yard near Liverpool's South Dock where, in 1778, he completed a commission for a privateer. However, he was a dreadful craftsman, and his client rejected the ship, named *Mentor*, which had been described as 'a sorry specimen of a ship, clumsy, ill-built, lopsided... with sailing qualities more suited to a hay stack than a smart privateer'. So, Baker decided to take advantage of the current trend, and he equipped the *Mentor* himself, complete with a fine array of cannon, and planned to set sail as a privateer.

However, because the vessel was so poorly built, and its sea-worthiness could not be guaranteed, the only crewmen he could attract were either incompetent or idle 'dock-side water-rats', or thieves and vagabonds sensing the opportunity for some easy gold. Of equal incompetence was a friend of Baker's, John Dawson, to whom he offered the job of captain.

Dawson was a man of limited experience at sea, but he was badly in debt and saw the voyage as a way of changing his circumstances. So, in the autumn of 1778, the *Mentor*, Captain Dawson, and his crew of ne'er-do-wells, ruffians, and scum set sail. Changing his mind about the risks at sea, Baker waved them off from the quayside!

On the 28 October 1778, completely by chance, *Mentor* came upon a ship that Dawson believed was a Spanish man o'war. He realised that, even with his ship's twenty-eight cannon, he would be vastly out-matched – especially when, through the telescope, he counted seventy-eight cannon on board the warship. Dawson was about to put about and sail away quickly but, fortunately, not every member of his crew was inept. The ship's carpenter now scanned the foreign ship, and reported that it was, in fact, French – the *Carnatic* – and that all its guns were dummies.

Suddenly much bolder, Dawson fired some warning shots across the *Carnatic*'s bows – and, to everyone's surprise, she immediately surrendered without a struggle.

The *Mentor*'s crew boarded *Carnatic* and claimed her as an English prize of war. To Dawson's amazement, when he took an inventory of her cargo he discovered that the ship was carrying vast quantities of exotic spices and other trade goods, worth £400,000: the value today would be more than £29 million. The cargo also included a box of diamonds, valued at more than £135,000 (almost £10 million at today's prices).

The news somehow reached Liverpool before the *Mentor* and, as she drew near the dockside of her home port, church bells were ringing out, and cheering crowds – which included the ecstatic Peter Baker – lined the wharf.

The *Mentor*'s crew were now rich men, and Baker was wealthy beyond his wildest dreams, buying the manor of Garston as a result. He also built himself a grand mansion, which local wags ironically named 'Carnatic Hall'. But he did not mind this at all, even adopting the name for his luxurious stately home.

But he did not stop there: *Mentor* went on to capture two more prizes, before finally foundering in a storm off Newfoundland, three years later. This loss, tragically, claimed the lives of all her company, with the sole exceptions of the captain, the mate, and the cabin-boy.

Still safe at home, Baker and his shipyard now prospered, and he went on to live a happy and very comfortable life in his mansion. Elected Mayor of Liverpool in 1795, Baker died in February the following year, while still in office, at the age of sixty-four.

In 1856, Letters of Marque were abolished across Europe, and the lucrative privateering trade was no more – but not before many Liverpudlians had made a great deal of money, and the town itself had benefitted from its profits.

AD 1770–1888

MOTHER REDCAP – THE SMUGGLER CHIEFTAINESS

Of Catastrophe, Caverns and Contraband

THE WATERS OF the Wirral coast, especially the Burbo and Hoyle Banks, are deadly and treacherous. High tides, turbulent and unpredictable storms, strong currents, and shifting sandbanks, were all part of the challenges that sailing ships had to face, coming into and out of the expanding port of Liverpool.

But, as if this wasn't enough of a risk to merchant ships sailing towards the safety of the town and its harbour, they also might have to contend with the threat provided by the people of Wallasey – especially during the seventeenth and eighteenth centuries.

During this period, what was then the small village of Wallasey was almost completely surrounded by bogs, marsh, and deadly quicksands – virtually cutting it off from the rest of the peninsular, unless one knew the safe pathways and tracks. Safe too from the eighteenth-century Customs inspectors – the Revenue Men – and the soldiers of the King who often accompanied them. Because of this isolation, the entire community of the district was free to become some of England's most ruthless wreckers and smugglers.

On dark and stormy nights in particular, with waves crashing over the decks of

heaving vessels, terrified sailors would try desperately to keep their small vessels from capsizing. Sails would be torn and ropes wrenched out of the hands of the men by the fierce winds. Their only light would come from the moon, and only then when it appeared briefly from behind the thick, black, ragged ribbons of cloud as they scudded across the sky.

'How far are we from the haven?' They would cry – hoping against hope to see the first light of the port of Liverpool.

Then they would see it! Faint at first, but then brighter and brighter – the welcoming yellow and golden lantern light of lamps being waved to guide them safely into harbour. Through the storm and the driving rain they would steer towards these reassuring and friendly lights!

But then, and far too late to put about, the horrified mariners would see the rocks and shoals off the Wallasey coast and know that all was lost, as their frail ships ploughed remorselessly on to certain catastrophe. Vessels would shatter and break themselves on the rocks; their guts spilling into the violent seas, along with their cargoes and their crews.

It was not friendly lanterns at all that had drawn them here, but the luring lights

A more innocent use: New Brighton is pictured here at the height of its fame as a beach resort, but before then it was an infamous haunt of smugglers.

The Red Noses, from which hidden caverns and tunnels lead under New Brighton and deep into the Wirral Peninsular.

51

In eighteenth- and nineteenth-century Liverpool, to avoid the perils of the press gangs – who literally abducted men and boys into forced service in the British Navy – sailors aboard merchant vessels and privateers would keep an ear open for the cry, 'Hawks abroad!', from people on both shores as they sailed into the River Mersey. Realising that this meant that the press gangs were at their vicious work, they would leave a skeleton crew aboard to bring the ship into harbour, whilst the rest of the crew would jump overboard and swim to the safety of Mother Redcap's inn.

Once their ship had been re-loaded, it would sail slowly past the Wallasey shore again, so that the sailors could swim out and climb back on board. This practice gave rise to the phrase 'jumping ship'.

of the Wallasey Wreckers, who were now racing down from the headlands and wading out in the waves. Crowds of men, women, and children would scavenge the shore with carts, barrows, horses, asses, and even oxen, which were used to draw timber, bales, boxes, or anything that the raging waters might have cast up.

As far as the authorities and the rest of the world were concerned, these were only simple fisherfolk, labourers, and farmers – but they were, in reality, greedy, vicious, and heartless people, for whom profit and escaping the royal troops and the Revenue Men were their sole aims. Virtually all of the inhabitants of this area – entire families and communities – were part of this nefarious trade, and they were very good at it.

Many a half-drowned sailor who had survived the wreck, whilst trying to obtain a footing and come safely to land, would be bludgeoned to death and cast back into the sea again – no one was left alive to tell the tale. Any corpses that washed up on the shore would be stripped of all coin or valuables and, if the rings on their fingers would not easily come off, then the wreckers would go to work with their knives or short axes. Clothes too would be stripped from the drowned seamen, leaving them naked in the waves – there was no compas-

sion here: money and contraband were at stake, and no other considerations applied.

So what did these wreckers and smugglers do with their plunder?

On the shoreline at what is now New Brighton, and the main location for these nefarious and bloody activities, are a line of rugged sandstone cliffs, known, because of the shapes and colours of the rock, as the 'Red Noses' and the 'Yellow Noses'. Great caves opened up in the cliff-face, connecting with a warren of tunnels and passages – natural and man-made – which still run deep into the peninsular. These caves have long since been hidden: the land has been deliberately raised to block them off, more than halving the height of the cliffs from their original level of at least 50ft above the shoreline.

The wreckers would drag their looted booty into this warren of caves and tunnels, and one of these passages in particular led to a tiny place further down the coast, almost opposite Liverpool, called Egremont. Here stood the only building for miles around: the tavern known as Mother Redcap's Inn.

Originally built in 1595, it was taken over, in the 1770s, by buxom and shrewd Polly 'Poll' Jones, known as 'Mother Redcap' because of the cap she habitually wore.

On what is now the corner of Caithness Drive, on Egremont Parade, this tavern became notorious as the haunt of rough, tough, rugged sailors and maritime folk – and of smugglers!

Poll brewed her own strong ale, which was itself a major attraction at the tavern, and she was very popular with local seafarers from both sides of the river. She would also look after a mariner's goods and gold for a small fee, keeping these safe in one of the caves beneath her inn until he returned from his next voyage. And Poll could be trusted – she never stole from the sailors.

But Mother Redcap was also said to be the leader of the Wallasey smugglers and wreckers, storing their ill-gotten gains beneath her tavern. Usually, though, contraband would only be held temporarily at Mother Redcap's, later being moved by people who knew the secret pathways across the quicksands, bogs, and marshes of Bidston Moss. They would make their way across the 'Jaw Bones' – a partly-submerged footbridge, made from the jawbones of a whale and covered in rough planks – to the Ring O' Bells Inn, in Bidston Village; today it is known as Stone Farm. Here, the booty would be 'divvied up' amongst the gang – once Poll had taken her cut, of course!

Nevertheless, it was always believed that she kept her own great stockpile of gold and loot in some secret vault below her tavern and, when Mother Redcap died, sometime in the mid-1800s, it surprised people that no such hoard was found.

Mother Redcap's Inn was rebuilt in 1888, when it was converted and re-designed as a café for local trippers and tourists. During this rebuilding, trapdoors, secret chambers, and passages were indeed discovered. The large yard at the rear was actually the roof of a sizeable cavern beneath the inn, made of great sandstone slabs, supported on beams, and disguised with earth and a manure pile. It was from this cave that the tunnel led to the Red and Yellow Noses, proving that the legends were true – and increasing the sale of 'teas, light refreshments, and minerals' in the process!

Becoming derelict in the 1960s, Mother Redcap's Café – the former haven for smugglers and wreckers – was itself wrecked when, in 1974, it was demolished. A residential home now stands on the site, named 'Mother Redcap's Nursing Home', and, whilst she is certainly neither a resident nor the proprietor, perhaps her spirit haunts the rooms at night, and perhaps, in some lost passage or cave, lies her long-lost 'buried treasure'.

BLOOD MONEY – THE TRIANGULAR TRADE

Suffering Humanity in Chains

SLAVERY HAD BEEN a normal and socially acceptable trade throughout Britain since 1553, when the first regular trading took place with Africa. By the late 1600s, Bristol had the monopoly, replacing London as the most significant British slave-trading port. Merchants from Bristol oversaw the exporting of slaves from West Africa to the Windward Islands and Virginia, and Liverpool wanted to take advantage of what was a very lucrative business.

Within fifty years, Liverpool had indeed overtaken Bristol and, although merchants in the town engaged in many other trades and commodities, involvement in the slave trade pervaded the whole port. Nearly all the principal merchants and citizens of Liverpool, including many of its mayors, were involved. Several of the town's MPs also invested in the trade and spoke strongly in its favour in Parliament.

The first recorded slaving ship to set sail from Liverpool was *The Liverpool Merchant*, which sold a cargo of 220 slaves in Barbados in 1700. Then, in 1737, Liverpool began to invest seriously in the trade. Vast fortunes were made for many Liverpool ship owners and, in 1771 alone, 105 ships sailed from Liverpool to West Africa, and

from there transported 28,200 slaves to the West Indies. In the town, slavery was known as the 'Triangular Trade', because of the three sea-routes it followed.

First, trade goods, such as pottery, jewellery, fabrics, and knives, would be shipped to the west coast of Africa. Here, these would be exchanged, with African slavers, for men, women, and children who had been abducted into captivity from their villages. In the holds of the same ships, these poor souls would then make the dreadful journey on the 'Middle Passage'; the second part of the triangle. This transported them from Africa to the slave plantations of the West Indies and the southern states of America.

Finally, the survivors of the voyage would be exchanged for rum, cotton, tobacco, and sugar cane. These commodities would then be shipped back to Liverpool, for processing, sale, and onward transportation to the rest of Britain and her Empire. But it was the Middle Passage that was the most fearsome part of the Triangular Trade.

At sea for up to eight weeks, crossing the Atlantic Ocean in all weathers, the slaves were packed tightly together in chains. Naked, on hard wooden shelves, and with no room to move, the sexes and ages were randomly mixed and families forced apart. Fed only on subsistence levels of gruel or thin soup; with no way to relieve themselves (other than where they lay); afflicted by sea-sickness, dysentery, and terror, the conditions were foul beyond belief. In fact, a fifth of all slaves died during the Atlantic crossing, and only 60 per cent of those who did make land survived for more than a year in captivity. Of those, most only lived into their thirties.

It is estimated that, from the middle of the fifteenth century to the end of the nineteenth century, more than 12 million Africans were kidnapped. In the eighteenth century alone, 6 million African slaves were transported to the American plantations. How many of these poor souls died during the process is, of course, unknown.

Shamefully, Britain had the largest slave-trading fleets, and Liverpool had now become the county's most 'successful' slave-trading port.

During the town's involvement in the trade, 1,360,000 African people were transported in over 5,000 voyages made by Liverpool vessels. Indeed, more than half of all slaves sold by English traders were the property of Liverpool merchants and, by the end of the eighteenth century, the town had 70 per cent of Britain's slave trade.

Small numbers of slaves, of both sexes and all ages, were brought to Liverpool and were occasionally sold at local auctions. These people were mostly used as house slaves for the more wealthy families in the town: black domestic servants in great houses were seen as a conspicuous sign of wealth at that time and, whilst some were paid wages and could leave their employers, others were treated as property, or as 'pets' or 'fashion statements'; particularly young boys. You may hear tales of shackles and iron rings, fastened to the walls of dock buildings in the city, but these stories have no basis in fact.

The marks of slavery shown in graphic form on the back of a slave. Four of every ten slaves died within a year of captivity. (Courtesy of the Library of Congress, Prints & Photographs Division, LC-USZ62-98515)

But then the attitude to slavery began to change in Britain and, in 1787, a petition for the suppression of the slave trade was handed to Parliament by some members of the Society of Friends (Quakers). Because of this action, in 1788, Liverpool Corporation formally declared its opposition to the Slave Trade. It is important to note that there was a large, vocal, and well-organised abolitionist movement in Liverpool, led by powerful merchants and philanthropists, such as William Roscoe, who were supported, significantly, by large numbers of influential and prominent women in the town.

Eventually, and following years of public meetings and acrimonious debate, and despite protectionism and downright ignorance throughout Britain, in 1807, an 'Act for the Abolition of The Transatlantic Slave Trade' was carried through Parliament. This outlawed the transportation of

The birthplace at Liverpool of William Roscoe, abolitionist.

slaves by British ships, thus beginning the end of the Triangular Trade. However, the subsequent 'Slavery Abolition Act' was not passed until 1830, and slavery across the British Empire was not finally stamped out until 1838.

The British Government ensured that former slave-ship, slave and plantation owners, and others who had interests vested in the trade, were generously compensated for their losses: former slaves received nothing for theirs.

Despite this removal of a highly lucrative source of revenue, the port of Liverpool and its maritime trade continued to thrive,

thanks to families such as the Rathbones, Holts, Rankins, and Bibbys. These were a new breed of entrepreneurial ship-owners, trading in a variety of commodities, other than in human bondage and exploitation. Such prominent individuals laid the foundation for Liverpool's massive expansion, and its more wholesome economic success during the nineteenth and early twentieth centuries. Indeed, Liverpool's peak of business growth was achieved in the half-century following abolition, and its highest population – 867,000 – was achieved in 1937.

Liverpool as a modern city, and as a community of diverse and multi-racial peoples, fully recognises this blight on our heritage.

However, many other British towns and cities played their part too, and also have the taint of slavery in their histories. These are places that provided the goods that were exchanged for the slaves, and included:

Pottery and earthenware – from Stoke and Staffordshire
Cheap jewellery – from Lancashire towns
Cotton and linen – from Manchester
Woollen goods – from Leeds and Bradford
Glassware – from St Helens
Knives and axes – from Sheffield

They were all culpable.

On 6 September 1781, the Liverpool slave ship *Zong*, outward bound from Africa and under the command of Captain Luke Collingwood, was, as was normal for such vessels, massively over-packed with its human cargo. So many slaves had already died, because of the appalling conditions on board, that Collingwood decided to throw a further 132 of them overboard, alive, so that he could claim compensation and cover his already significant financial losses.

His claim was denied, but the actual murder of the slaves was not an issue during his subsequent trial – only the captain's attempted fraud.

THE TRAGEDY OF THE COLLAPSING CHURCH TOWER

The Crushed Children of The Seamen's Church

IN THE ATTRACTIVE gardens at the corner of Chapel Street stands Liverpool parish church, dedicated to 'Our Lady and Saint Nicholas'. This has been known, for generations, as 'The Seamen's Church'.

Chapel Street is one of Liverpool's original seven streets, laid out by King John after 1207. It was named for the first place of Christian worship in Liverpool, which once stood on a site very close to the present church. This was the ancient 'Chapel of St Mary del Key' (or 'Quay'), which was once right on the water's edge and had been a place of pilgrimage from the very earliest times.

As the small town began to expand, the chapel needed to grow too, so, in 1361, a new and larger church was consecrated, dedicated to 'Saint Mary and Saint Nicholas'. This now stood a little further back from the river, on land granted to 'the burgesses of the town' by the then Duke of Lancaster, John of Gaunt (1340–1399).

The new church consisted of a chancel, a nave, a western tower, and a large aisle. John of Gaunt had known the original Chapel well, and he now paid for the building of a chantry, adjacent to the main altar, in the new church. A chantry was a special chapel, maintained by an endowment, in which masses were chanted for the soul of the founder, or for somebody named by the founder.

Saint Mary and Saint Nicholas' church now replaced the old chapel as the place where seafarers would come to pray before setting off on another perilous voyage. The families and friends of these sailors would come to pray here too, whilst their loved ones were at sea, to ask for their safe return.

Between 1673 and 1718, the building was added to and extended at various times and, in 1746, a spire was added to the tower. Then, in 1774, the church was almost entirely rebuilt, now becoming more commonly known as the church of 'Our Lady and St Nicholas'.

The building not only had a human significance but also a strategic one. In 1759, a battery of fourteen guns was placed in the cemetery, where the gardens now stand, to protect the port from attacks by French privateers. This was still a time when the River Mersey washed right up to the wall of the church, and before George's Dock was built, in 1767, on the place where the Royal Liver Building now stands.

The church continued to play a major part in the life of the town, and its Sunday

57

services were always fully attended. However, by the beginning of the nineteenth century the building was in need of serious maintenance. In fact, there had been repeated warnings that the spire was unsafe. But then, on Sunday, 11 February 1810, as people were assembling for Sunday morning service, the bells were being rung particularly vigorously.

The noise and vibration was too much for the badly-maintained structure, and an eye-witness describes what happened next:

I was standing in St Nicholas churchyard, in company with two old friends. We were waiting the arrival of the congregation... the second bells were chiming. Our conversation had turned upon the benefits which a good sound Christian education must confer upon the lower classes of society... Our remarks had been evoked by the neat appearance of the children of the Moorfields Schools, who had just passed near where we stood, as they entered the church.

Just as he had finished speaking, we heard, as if above us, a smart crack. On looking round to ascertain the cause, a sight burst upon our view, that none who witnessed it could ever forget.

The instant we turned, we beheld the church tower give way, on the southwest side, and immediately afterwards the spire fell with a frightful and appalling crash into the body of the building. The spire seemed at first to topple over, and then it dropped perpendicularly like a pack of cards into a solid heap, burying everything, as may be supposed, below it.

There were many persons in the churchyard, waiting to enter the sacred edifice, and, like ourselves, were struck dumb with horror and dismay at the frightful catastrophe. We were soon aroused to a state of consciousness, and inaction gave way to exertion. In a very short time, the noise of the crash had brought hundreds of persons into the churchyard to ascertain the cause.

Amidst the rising dust were heard the dreadful screams of the poor children who had become involved in the ruins; and not long after, their screams were added to by the frantic exclamations of parents and friends who, in an incredibly short time, had hurried to the scene of the disaster.

Crowds of people rushed into the churchyard, some hurrying to and fro, scarcely knowing what to fear or what to do. That the children were to be exhumed was an immediate thought, and as immediately carried into execution.

Men of all ranks were seen, quite regardless of their Sunday clothes, busily employed in removing the ruins – gentlemen, merchants, tradesmen, shopmen and apprentices, willingly aiding the sturdy labourers in their good work, and, in a short time, first one little sufferer, and then another, was dragged out from the mass of stone and brick and timber that lay in a confused heap.

Twenty-eight little ones were at length brought out, of whom twenty-three were dead; five were alive, and were taken to the Infirmary, but of these, only three survived. They were horribly maimed, and so disfigured that they were scarcely recognizable. These twenty-eight poor little bodies were at first laid in rows in the churchyard to be claimed by their parents and friends, many of whom were to be seen running to and fro looking distracted with the great calamity that had befallen them.

Of all the pitiable sights I ever beheld, the sight of these little things laid on the grass was the most piteous; and as one by one they were claimed and taken away – in some instances parents claiming two, and in one instance, three children – the utmost sympathy was felt for those who had been so suddenly bereft.

During the first outbreak of plague in Liverpool, there were so many victims that there was nowhere to bury them near the ancient Chapel of St Mary del Key. So, in 1361, a special Bishop's Licence was granted to create a new burial ground around the building. All signs of this cemetery have now gone, to be replaced by beautiful gardens; but it is very likely that hundreds of plague victims still lie there, beneath the tidy lawns and the neat pathways.

If the collapse of the tower had taken place fifteen minutes later, the death toll would have been far greater; as it was, and in addition to the children (who were all little girls), only twenty or so people had taken their seats at the rear of the church. But whilst the children were in the front pews, these others were at the back, and so were able to escape safely out of the rear door. By some miracle the bell-ringers all escaped unscathed too, but the entirely preventable loss of those young girls brought shame and dishonour on the church authorities.

Because of this shocking tragedy, the Chester architect Thomas Harrison was brought in to redesign and rebuild the tower. In 1815 the work was completed, and the new 120ft high tower, with spectacular flying buttresses, was surmounted by a beautiful – but much more lightweight – lantern spire. This is a further 60ft high. Since 1916, Our Lady and St Nicholas' has been the parish church of Liverpool, but the events leading to the tragic deaths of twenty-five children have never been forgotten.

THE HOPE STREET BODY SNATCHERS

The Corpses in the Casks

N JANUARY 1822, the Revd James McGowan opened a day school for boys, on land at the rear of his house on Hope Street. Entrance into the building, which had a large cellar with separate access, was from the alley alongside the property, in Back Canning Street.

The school accommodated around fifty children, aged between four and sixteen, and was quite popular. However, McGowan had five daughters, all growing rapidly, so to supplement his income, he decided to rent out the spacious empty cellar beneath the schoolroom. Someone who seemed to be the ideal tenant soon appeared, in the person of a John Henderson. Henderson explained that he wished to set up a cooperage, making large casks and barrels. He told the reverend that he was in the business of exporting fish oil, so this would be the perfect premises for him.

He did not say that he intended to fill his casks with oil in the cellar, but when, some weeks later, a dreadful smell began to waft its way out from under the schoolroom, it was assumed that this was the reason. Over the coming weeks, though, the smell grew considerably stronger – but the schoolmaster still needed the extra money, and did not want to evict his tenant. The smell also

seemed to come intermittently, and was only offensive when there was no wind, so he decided that he, and his pupils in the schoolroom above, could put up with it.

Throughout 1826, Henderson and his two associates used the cellar regularly, but were quiet and caused no other problems. However, they did not welcome interruption or interest from either the schoolchildren or passing neighbours; they even painted over the cellar windows so people could not see in. 'People were entitled to their privacy,' reasoned the schoolmaster, so he did not question this. Not so the young schoolboys, however, whose natural curiosity got the better of them.

They took great delight in watching great sacks of salt being taken down the steps into the cellar and, a few days later, huge, heavy casks being brought up and loaded onto horse-drawn carts waiting in the street.

'What's in them barrels then, Mister?' One or two bolder children asked the workmen one day.

'Fish oil,' came the terse response.

'Is that what the stink is then, Mister?'

'Yes,' was the equally blunt reply.

'What's it for then?'

'It's goin' down to the docks, and then gets shipped up to Scotland. Now, enough of your questions! Move on. Leave us to our work!'

But this only temporarily quelled the curiosity of the children – especially when, over the next few days, the smell from the cellar became very much worse: so much so that people now avoided walking down that end of Hope Street and Back Canning Street. Poor Reverend McGowan began to get vociferous complaints from his neighbours. But, just as he was about to admit that the situation was unacceptable, and that his smelly tenants had to go, the matter resolved itself.

It was approaching evening-time on 9 October 1826 when a carter arrived on Hope Street with instructions to collect a consignment of three very large casks labelled 'bitter salts', and to take them down to Liverpool docks. From here, they would be taken aboard the trading vessel *Latona*, which, in a couple of day's time, was due to set sail for Leith, in Scotland.

The carter stood and watched as the workmen brought the casks up from the cellar and hoisted them up onto the flat open bed of his cart – he was told not to go down the cellar himself, but that suited him as it made his job easier. It was a breezy evening, which was probably why the smell from the casks was not too bad,

and why the crewmen of the *Latona* lowered them into the ship's hold without comment or complaint. But this state of affairs did not last.

In the morning, the ship's crew went to their captain to complain that they had not had a wink of sleep because of the now dreadful stench coming from the hold. The captain went down with his men to discover its source, and they realised immediately that it was coming from the great barrels.

'Break 'em open, lads,' the captain instructed. 'Let's see what's makin' such a God-awful reek.'

Covering their noses and mouths with handkerchiefs, they set about the lids with axes, only to back away in horror and revulsion when they saw what was inside them: bodies! Naked, human bodies – eleven of them, packed in salt.

The police were called and an investigation began. This led the officers to the house, schoolroom, and cellar in Hope Street. When the policemen made their way down the steps, accompanied by the shocked and innocent Revd McGowan, they could not believe their eyes – or their noses.

There, in various states of decomposition, were the naked corpses of men, women, boys, and girls; some in barrels and some in heaps on the floor. Most horrifying

---

Near to Hope Street is Rodney Street. This is said to be haunted by the ghost of wealthy William McKenzie, who died in 1851. He had instructed that his body should to be interred, sitting at a card table, inside a pyramid-shaped tomb, in the graveyard of St Andrew's church. This was because McKenzie believed that this would prevent the Devil from snatching his soul, after he had sold it to 'Old Nick' in exchange for success at cards.

The contract had specified that the Devil could take him once he had been buried underground; as he never was, the Devil was cheated. Perhaps this is why William's ghost prowls the streets of Liverpool.

of all, though, was a cask full of babies, slowly pickling in salt-water.

At the subsequent inquest, in Liverpool, it was confirmed that, whilst these unfortunate people had all died of natural causes, they had been victims of what became known as 'The Hope Street Body Snatchers'. Each had probably been dug up, in the dead of night, from the graveyard that served the workhouse at the top of nearby Brownlow Hill.

Whilst Henderson and his accomplices had gone into hiding in the town, the inquest also revealed that they had been involved in a very lucrative business. The corpses they had exhumed were being used by medical students and doctors, in Scotland and elsewhere, for dissection and experimentation. At the time, this was not in itself illegal, which is why the body-snatchers probably felt no need to leave the town. But the practice was abhorrent to ordinary people, who expected to stay buried when finally laid in the ground.

By now, the case had become so notorious that the grave-robbers were soon identified and arrested. However, because the law said that this was only a minor offence – life and death being so cheap in those days – they were each only sentenced to twelve months in Kirkdale Gaol and the payment of a fine. But what of the pickled people in the barrels?

When the bodies in the cellar were added to the ones from the ship, the total came to about thirty-three corpses, and the inquest ordered that these should all be re-buried immediately. However, to save on expense and inconvenience, the authorities decided that a mass grave would suffice; back in the graveyard from where they had all been dug up. To save even more money, it was decided not to buy individual coffins, but to pack them all back in the barrels again, and bury them in those.

At the graveside, and without any funeral service or semblance of respect, the barrels were rolled down a broad plank into the pit. But when they hit the bottom the casks split apart, spilling out their grisly contents. They were quickly sprinkled with quicklime and covered over with earth: their final resting place unmarked. The bodies may lie there still, under the buildings that now form part of the modern campus of the University of Liverpool.

AD 1830

RUN OVER BY A 'ROCKET'

A Tragic Claim To Fame

L IVERPOOL HAS BEEN the 'first' at a number of remarkable discoveries and achievements, and one of the most significant is that, in 1830, the world's first passenger train, drawn by a steam locomotive, travelled from the town to Manchester. Soon, railways were crisscrossing Britain, and driving ever onward its industrial and commercial revolution. But that remarkable inaugural day was marred by a dreadful tragedy.

It was the 18 September, and in the early afternoon the bunting was out and the bands played. Great crowds of excited people thronged the railway tracks at Crown Street Station, in the Liverpool district of Edge Hill, as a convoy of trains pulled out on their journey to our sister city.

The Duke of Wellington (1769–1852), who was Prime Minister at the time and travelling with other VIP guests, was in his own carriage on the southern track. This was being pulled by the locomotive *Northumbrian*. On the parallel northern track was a procession of trains, each pulled by different locomotives. These were *Phoenix*, *North Star*, *Dart*, *Comet*, *Arrow*, and the *Meteor*. Leading the cavalcade was the *Rocket*, which had been designed and built by George Stephenson and his son Robert.

This had won a competition, held the previous year at the Rainhill Steam Trials, to find the most successful design for a new form of locomotive engine.

The train that carried all the distinguished guests had stopped to take on water halfway along the route, at the

Wellington, who shook the hand of the world's first victim of a railway accident.

63

Parkfield Watering-Station, about 17 miles out of Liverpool. Amongst the important people in the Prime Minister's special train was the local MP, William Huskisson (born 1770), accompanied by his wife. During the 1820s, Huskisson had been one of the primary backers of the Liverpool and Manchester Railway and, in 1826, had helped to secure the legislation that would allow construction to begin. As the dignitaries' train had stopped, this provided an opportunity for the trains and carriages full of people on the northern track to pass by and get a look at the 'great and the good'.

At this point, the VIPs got out of their open-topped carriages to socialise and stretch their legs – despite being warned against this by railway officials. The Duke remained in his carriage, acknowledging greetings from his fellow travellers.

William Huskisson thought that, because of the general mood of good will, this would be a perfect opportunity to heal a long-standing rift between himself and the Prime Minister. So he made his way between the two lines of railway tracks, up to the Duke's carriage.

Warmly welcomed by his political adversary, the Liverpool MP opened the carriage door in order to shake the Duke's hand, which was now being extended towards him. But then Huskisson realised that the other trains, led by George Stephenson's *Rocket*, were advancing towards him along the parallel track, only a few feet away from him.

All the people who had been walking around quickly began to scramble back aboard their own carriages, leaving Huskisson as the last person standing on the ground, with his hand on the open carriage door. It was clear to observers that he was too close to the approaching locomotive, and the engineer shouted out to him,

'Hi, sir! Stand clear! Stand clear!'

At the same time, people called to him from his carriage,

'Mr Huskisson, sir, the locomotive, it's

upon you, sir!' But this only confused him.

As he struggled to pull himself up into the Duke's carriage, his strength failed and, already weakened by a recent illness, he lost control of the carriage door, which swung outwards, knocking him into the path of the oncoming *Rocket*.

The unfortunate MP was struck by the engine and he fell to the ground. As he did so, his left knee was thrown across the northern track in a bent position, and the wheels of the succeeding carriages crushed his thigh and leg – producing a loud 'crunching' sound, according to eye-witnesses, and 'squeezing it almost to a jelly'!

One of the eyewitnesses to the accident was a reporter from *Gore's Liverpool Advertiser*. He takes up the story:

> Though we distinctly heard Mr Huskisson shriek as the carriage passed, we had no idea that any serious mischief had happened... Several of the Directors, and of the distinguished visitors from the Duke of Wellington's carriage, immediately crowded around to offer their services...
>
> Mr Huskisson said,
>
> 'Where is Mrs Huskisson? I have met my death. God forgive me.'
>
> 'The Northumbrian engine, and the carriage which contained the band, were detached from the state carriage; and Mr Huskisson, having been carefully placed on a board, was carried upon men's shoulders, and deposited in the carriage of the band...
>
> Mr Stephenson, taking charge of the engine, set out towards Manchester at a most terrific rate, travelling from the place where the accident happened to Eccles Bridge, at the rate of 34 miles an hour...

At Eccles, the mortally injured man was taken to the local vicarage, whilst George Stephenson continued with the *Northumbrian*, to find medical assistance at the Manchester station. By this time, it was about four o'clock in the afternoon.

AD1889

Flypaper Arsenic, and Medical Bags

Was Jack the Ripper a Scouser?

O, she is fallen
Into a pit of ink, that the wide sea,
Hath drops too few to wash her clean again.

MUCH ADO ABOUT NOTHING.—Act IV., Sc. 1.

Mr James Maybrick.

Florence Maybrick at the time of her trial.

IN AIGBURTH, A leafy southern suburb of Liverpool, is Riversdale Road. Near its junction with Aigburth Road, and opposite Liverpool Cricket Club, stands the nineteenth-century mansion known as Battlecrease House. Now converted into separate apartments, this was once the grand home of wealthy cotton broker James Maybrick (1838-1889), and his wife, Florence (1862-1941).

Florence was an American, and had been sailing to a new life in Britain aboard the SS *Baltic*, in 1880. It was whilst at sea that she met James. She was a bright and attractive woman, and he was a handsome and charming man: romance blossomed; troths were plighted; and a wedding was planned. Once in Britain they married, and eventually settled in Liverpool at Battlecrease House. But the gilt on their relationship was soon to tarnish.

James was a man of eccentric hobbies; he had a morbid interest in illnesses, medicines, and potions. He would spend hours in his laboratory in their large house, mixing up strange concoctions, and was frequently to be seen walking around the streets of Liverpool and London, where he also had business interests, carrying a small black medical bag, said to contain an array of surgical knives and scalpels, as well as other medical equipment.

Florence was soon to discover what friends and neighbours seemed to have already known for some time: that her husband had a dark and unpleasant side to his personality. He began to become increasingly aggressive and extremely short-tempered with his wife, and theirs was no longer a happy marriage. Nevertheless, the couple had two children, but this did not improve their relationship.

Then, in the early spring of 1889, James became ill. He could not eat, endured all the worst symptoms of gastric poisoning and, after suffering and lingering for many weeks, he died. The doctor who attended him was puzzled, and the circumstances of James's death were soon the subject of much

White Star liner SS Baltic *at Liverpool Landing Stage: the Maybricks met on board.*

local gossip: so much so that the police decided to mount an investigation. Before long, this resulted in Florence being charged with the murder of her husband, allegedly by using arsenic, which she had scraped from flypapers, to slowly poison the food of her odious spouse.

Later in the same year, Florence appeared at Liverpool Crown Court, which was then in St George's Hall. The trial became the sensation of the decade, attracting vast crowds of spectators and extensive press coverage.

And, as the details of her life with James began to be revealed in court, Florence found herself the subject of great public sympathy. Despite this, on 7 August 1889, she was found guilty of murder and sentenced to be hanged.

There was a public outcry, and a press campaign was mounted in her favour. Two weeks after the trial had ended Florence's sentence was commuted to life imprisonment, but Queen Victoria refused to endorse a reduction in the allocated prison term, despite many appeals for her to do so. However, Florence

Maybrick only spent fourteen years in jail, because once Edward VII had succeeded to the throne he requested that her sentence be commuted. And so, in 1904, Florence gained her release.

She moved to America and lived there for the remainder of her life, coming back to Liverpool on a number of occasions, one of which was to attend the Grand National Steeplechase. Eventually, in 1941, Florence Maybrick died in America at the age of eighty-one, where she had been living her final years as a complete recluse.

The year before the murder of James Maybrick, throughout 1888, the names of five women – and the dreadful circumstances of their deaths – filled every newspaper in the country: Mary Anne Nichols; Annie Chapman; Elizabeth 'Long Liz' Stride; Catharine Eddowes; and Mary Jane Kelly. All were victims of the brutal murderer the world had come to know as 'Jack the Ripper'.

These 'Whitechapel Murder' victims had all been working girls in the East End of London, and had fallen prey to the knife of 'the Ripper'. First, their throats had been cut; then, with surgical precision, horrific mutilations had been carried out on their bodies. Annie Chapman's entrails had been pulled out and 'displayed' across her body,

Battlecrease House.

Opposite *The marriage certificate of*
Florence and James Maybrick, July 1881.

These pages *Outside St George's Hall,*
where thousands of Liverpudlians awaited
the verdict of the Maybrick trial in 1889.
(Courtesy of the Library of Congress,
LC-DIG-ppmsc-08555)

1881. Marriage solemnized at the Church in the Parish of St. James's, Westminster, in the County of ~~London~~ Middlesex

No.	When Married	Name and Surname	Age	Condition	Rank or Profession	Residence at time of Marriage	Father's Name and Surname	Rank or Profession of Father
327	July 27 1881	James Maybrick / Florence Elizabeth Chandler	full / a minor	Bachelor / Spinster	Esquire	S. James's / Paris	William Maybrick / William George Chandler	Gentleman (dec) / Banker (dec)

Married in the Church, according to the Rites and Ceremonies of the Established Church, by Licence or after

This Marriage was solemnised between us. | James Maybrick / Florence Elizabeth Chandler | in the Presence of us. | Michael Maybrick / Baroness Caroline E von Roques | by me. J Dyer Tovey Preacher & Assistant

I hereby certify that the above is a true Extract from the Register Book of Marriages belonging to the Parish of St. James's, Westminster.

Witness my Hand this 28th Day of April 1902

On 10 October 1888, a report in a Canadian newspaper, *The Globe*, reported that a new investigation into the Ripper killings was being undertaken by Scotland Yard.

Detectives had gone to Liverpool to follow a lead about a businessman who regularly travelled between the town and London, habitually carrying a black medical bag; he frequented the 'low districts' of East London. Could this be further evidence that James Maybrick was indeed Jack the Ripper?

and Catharine Eddowes' face had been left almost unrecognisable.

Jack the Ripper was never identified or brought to justice.

But then, in 1992, an unemployed scrap-metal dealer from Liverpool named Michael Barrett announced that he had come into possession of the authentic diary of a man declaring himself to be 'the Whitechapel Murderer' – the official name for 'Jack'.

Unsigned, this is a record of the exact details of the murders, plus another two killings, so far unidentified. Written in incredible detail and never referring to himself as 'Jack', or indeed by any other name, the author describes his emotions and the methods of his murders of the tragic women. He also gives much information about the rest of his life, sufficient to match those of James Maybrick.

Could it be that the reason the law never caught up with 'The Ripper' was that his wife, Florence, got to him first? Had she discovered her husband's other life, and decided to mete out justice herself? She never said so, and we are unlikely to ever know for sure. Many people firmly believe the diary to be authentic, whilst just as many think it is an elaborate hoax. Whatever the truth may be, James Maybrick now lies in Anfield Cemetery, just one of the candidates for the name and crimes of 'Jack the Ripper'.

Every day, without realising it, thousands of passengers on modern trains pass the site of Huskisson's accident at Parkside. A memorial was placed here at the time and it still stands, bearing an inscription, part of which reads:

'The accident changed a moment of the noblest exultation and triumph that science and genius had ever achieved
into one of desolation and mourning...'

William Huskisson.

Meanwhile, Huskisson was losing massive amounts of blood, and was failing fast. When the surgeons eventually arrived at the vicarage, they decided not to amputate, as this was bound to kill him, so he was given large doses of laudanum. This did little to relieve the dreadful agony he was suffering. Huskisson then took hold of the arm of one of the surgeons, a Mr Whatton, and spoke to him.

Here, the reporter takes up the narrative once more:

'I wish you to tell me candidly what you think of my case.'

Mr Whatton replied: 'It is a very bad one, and I fear, sir, that you cannot survive.'

Mr Huskisson rejoined, 'No, that I have fully made up my mind to, from the first; but how long do you think I have to live?'

The answer was, 'It is impossible to say exactly; but probably not more than four, five, or at most six hours.'

'Thank you,' said Mr Huskisson, and terminated the conversation.'

William Huskisson dictated his last will and, with his wife, he took the sacrament, although his breathing was by now much laboured. Shortly after this, the dying man said, 'I hope I have lived the life of a Christian,' and then thanked the surgeons for, 'their kind attentions to him'.

As the newspaper then reports;

Mr Huskisson took an affectionate leave of the sorrowing friends who surrounded his bedside, and a most tender farewell of his devoted wife, and precisely at nine o'clock, expired.

William Huskisson was a much-respected man in Liverpool, and throughout Britain, even though his campaigns for radical new policies, such as Catholic emancipation, made him the target of much vitriol – hence this original conflict with the Prime Minister. However, Huskisson's death, and the manner in which it occurred on such an otherwise illustrious day, shocked the nation. The public subscription that was rapidly taken up was sufficient to erect his magnificent tomb and mausoleum, which now stands in the centre of St James's Cemetery. This marks his life, and commemorates him as the world's first railway fatality.

THE MOLE OF EDGE HILL AND THE GATEWAY TO HELL

The Naked Demon Navvies

UNDERGROUND LIVERPOOL IS a labyrinth of tunnels; most are natural, but many are man-made, such as those constructed by Joseph Williamson, the 'Mole of Edge Hill'.

Joseph was born on 10 March 1769. Where is uncertain, but it is known that he moved to Liverpool from Warrington in 1780. He was a very poor young man, but he entered the tobacco and snuff business of Richard Tate, and was to go on to make his fortune. Joseph was diligent and industrious, and he rose rapidly through the ranks of business, continuing to work for Thomas Tate, the son of Richard, after his original employer had died.

In 1802, he married the boss's daughter, Elizabeth Tate. This was a shrewd move, and he went on to buy out the Tate firm a year later, soon becoming an extremely wealthy tobacco merchant.

Always an eccentric, on his wedding day – and as soon as the vicar had made the pronouncement of marriage – he told his wife to go home and get his dinner ready, leapt onto his horse, and galloped off to join the Liverpool Hunt, still in his wedding outfit. His appearance was described as being 'uncommonly grand', and it elicited much encouraging comment from his fellow Hunt members.

However, he was not usually a smart dresser, and Williamson's preferred everyday outfit was a battered beaver hat, an old patched brown coat, corduroy breeches, and hobnailed boots. Nevertheless, he was known throughout the town as being a kindly, but nonetheless 'odd' character. But then, from about 1806, Williamson's renowned peculiarities took a very specific turn.

Edge Hill at that time was 'out in the country' and largely uninhabited and, from Williamson's house, he would have had clear views of the River Mersey. However, Joseph did not look outwards; he began to look down instead and, starting from the cellar of his house in Mason Street, he began to excavate a series of subterranean passages and huge underground halls. These were to become his underground 'kingdom'.

Over the next thirty-five years, until 1840, Williamson spent £100,000 paying local unemployed men and soldiers returning from the Napoleonic Wars to extend what he had already begun, by excavating a vast network of useless tunnels and rooms in the sandstone under the district.

And so, at various depths between 10ft and 50ft below the surface, the tunnels began to riddle the area, in all directions from Mason Street and Smithdown Lane.

As well as the tunnels and passageways, there are vast vaults. These are between 30ft and 40ft wide, and some are over 50ft in height. There are also traps, pits, and chasms, all built for unknown purposes. Many tunnels are simply blank-walled or circular passages that lead to nothing more than a dead-end, or which bring you back on yourself in a meaningless journey.

Maybe Joseph was simply a genuine philanthropist? He certainly provided gainful, if somewhat pointless employment to hundreds of local men, and so supported their families who otherwise might have starved. Because of this he gained the soubriquet 'King of Edge Hill', from a grateful local community.

And his men worked willingly and happily for him, even in what must have been exceptionally difficult and uncomfortable physical conditions. When one considers that his entire workforce's labour

Lime Street, pictured when the railway age was at its height. The new terminus that George Stevenson was tunnelling towards was here – but he bumped into the Mole King before he could reach it. This view shows the London & North Western Hotel for travellers on the new lines. It is now a block of student flats.

was manual, with only picks, shovels, and barrows, and that their digging was carried out only by the light of candles and tallow lamps, then this really puts the mammoth nature of the task into a very human perspective. However, ever the caring employer, Williamson would often ply his workers with free barrels of ale or porter, as well as wages.

One of the many stories told about this unusual man is that, in 1836, whilst his men were working on his passages and tunnels under Edge Hill, the great engineer George Stephenson was digging a tunnel too. His was a large, arched railway tunnel for two lines of track, built to connect the Edge Hill station with a new terminus in the town centre, at Lime Street. What neither Stephenson nor Williamson knew was that their tunnels were getter ever closer together – the engineer's in the ground just above the Mole's!

Whilst Stephenson's men were organised, professional 'navvies', working with the latest tools and equipment and dressed in hard-wearing working clothes,

Inside Williamson's tunnels.

> The eccentric Williamson once invited a large group of wealthy and important people to dine with him. To their surprise, he sat them down on plain wooden benches in front of rough wooden tables. He then served ordinary pewter bowls full of simple bacon and bean stew. Most were affronted and stormed off. To those who stayed, Joseph said,
> 'You are my true friends, follow me!'
> And he led them into a glorious dining hall and fed them all a sumptuous banquet.

Williamson's men were somewhat disorganised, amateur excavators, working in confined and extremely hot spaces.

To preserve what few garments these poor men possessed, and to make it easier to work, many of Williamson's diggers worked either fully or semi-naked. Sweating profusely, and with the air full of dust from the diggings, the men's bodies were soon covered with layers of yellow and brown sandstone powder. This gave their skin an other-worldly glow in the glittering light of the lanterns and lamps.

All the while, the two tunnels were getting closer and closer. Then, without any warning, the ground in Stephenson's tunnel gave way beneath his shocked navvies. They fell only a few feet into Williamson's tunnel but, when they picked themselves up and looked around, they all began screaming: they had obviously fallen into Hell! The astonished men were completely surrounded by large, muscular, naked, sweaty, dirty Demons; all glowing orange and surrounded by flickering flames, and wielding pickaxes and pikes!

Fortunately, as the fall was only a matter of a few feet, no one was injured – just very frightened. But it took quite a few minutes before both gangs of men realised what had happened and who everyone actually was. It also took more than just a few flagons of ale to calm everyone down after that experience! Indeed, Stephenson's men required a lot of persuading before agreeing to return to work at all.

Williamson's comment to the great railway engineer at the time was typical of a Scouser: he simply told Stephenson that he 'had no idea how to build tunnels' but that he, Joseph Williamson, the King of Edge Hill, 'could give you lessons in that polite art'.

Joseph's long-suffering wife, Elizabeth, died in 1822 and, as a grieving reaction to this he threw himself into his tunnelling with greater vigour, and some say that he very rarely came above ground after this time. Williamson himself died in 1840, aged seventy. He was buried, with his wife and her family, in the Tate family vault in St Thomas's church, where they had married thirty-eight years earlier. This stood at the corner of Paradise Street and Park Lane. In 1905, the church was demolished and, to accommodate the changing road layout, some of the graves were removed, but not the Tate vault.

This now lies, with Joseph still in it, under a memorial garden close by the Liverpool ONE retail complex. This commemorates all those who were buried in this former churchyard, including the Mole – The King – of Edge Hill.

AD 1845

OF POTATOES AND PESTILENCE

The Great Hunger

THE EXPLOITATION OF the Irish by the British goes back to medieval times: all the way back, in fact, to King John, who created his new town of 'Leverpul' so that he could invade Ireland from here.

This oppression continued during the Tudor and Stuart monarchies, and on through the English Civil War (1642–51). It reached a peak during the time of Cromwell and the Commonwealth, when the brutality of the invading and occupying armies was both notorious and catastrophic.

Exploitation of the Catholic Irish peasantry persisted through to the eighteenth and nineteenth centuries, when the British Crown granted vast Irish estates to Protestant absentee landlords. These aristocrats were only interested in extracting as much wealth from their estates as possible without putting anything back into the local economy or community.

Ireland is a fertile country and large quantities of wheat and other crops were being produced. However, the vast bulk of this produce was exported to England for the enrichment of the titled, Protestant estate owners. These exports also included most of the livestock: this would either be shipped back, live, to Britain to be slaugh-

tered or, after being killed in Ireland, would be transported as salted carcasses. Both would find their way to English butchers and the dining tables of the wealthy.

The Irish peasantry never had access to any of this produce, and they could not have found the money to pay for it even if they had been allowed to buy it. This left only potatoes for the Irish people to live on – and, by 1840, this was literally the only food for almost half of Ireland's 8 million people. But then an almost nationwide blight completely ruined the potato crop.

Without warning, in September 1845, the leaves on potato plants suddenly turned black and shrivelled, and then began to rot. This process produced a foul stench, described at the time as being, 'like the miasma of death that washes the mortuary corpses'.

An airborne fungus (*phytophthora infestans*) – unknowingly carried into Britain on ships from North America – was now blowing across the Irish Sea from England. The blight then spread quickly throughout the potato fields around Dublin, and the plants then fermented, providing food for the mould to thrive on. As the spores rapidly multiplied, the winds then carried the pestilence all around the country: a single contaminated potato plant could infect thousands more in just a few days. This caused dreadful suffering.

An eye-witness report read:

My hand trembles while I write. The scenes of human misery and degradation we witnessed still haunt my imagination, with the vividness and power of some horrid and tyrannous delusion, rather than the features of a sober reality.

We entered a cabin.

Stretched in one dark corner, scarcely visible, from the smoke and rags that covered them, were three children huddled together, lying there because they were too weak to rise.

Pale and ghastly, their little limbs – on removing a portion of the filthy covering – were perfectly emaciated – eyes sunk, voice gone, and evidently in the last stage of actual starvation.

Crouched over the turf embers was another form, wild and all but naked, scarcely human in appearance. It stirred not, nor noticed us.

On some straw, soddened upon the ground and moaning piteously, was a shrivelled old woman, imploring us to give her something – baring her limbs partly, to show how the skin hung loose from the bones, as soon as she attracted our attention.

Above her, on something like a ledge, was a young woman, with sunken cheeks – a mother I have no doubt – who scarcely raised her eyes in answer to our enquiries, but pressed her hand upon her forehead, with a look of unutterable anguish and despair.

The 'Great Irish Potato Famine' killed 25 per cent of the Irish population – almost 1 million Irish men, women, and children. Two million more people emigrated to America – most of these coming through Liverpool.

Starving Ireland petitioning America for aid.(Library of Congress, LC-USZ62-103220)

Those that could not afford to continue their journey to either the New World or other parts of Britain – and there were tens of thousands of them – were forced to remain in Liverpool. This put intolerable pressures on what was an already heavily overburdened town, and the existing infrastructure could not cope. The result of this was that thousands of victims of the Irish Famine found themselves in conditions no better than those they had left behind.

Most of these people were forced to live, at best, in squalid, disease-ridden rooms, cellars, and court dwellings (densely-packed and overcrowded blocks of rooms built around a communal yard); or, at worst, on the streets as starving beggars. Across Liverpool, this new, rapidly expanding and dependant population exponentially increased the geographical spread of disease and poverty.

Settling largely in the northern districts of Vauxhall and Kirkdale in the town, these mainly Catholic Irish immigrants – although many of them were also Protestant – brought with them their religious beliefs and their politics. The Irish Potato Famine had scarred the hearts and minds of the Liverpool Irish, as well as their bodies.

This produced extremely deep feelings of resentment and distrust toward the British, especially the Government, whom the Irish held to be completely responsible for their suffering and for centuries of exploitation.

But now, the Protestants of Liverpool saw their religion and culture being threatened by the sheer weight of numbers of Catholics, in what they regarded as 'their' town. By 1886, the sectarian geography of the town had been established, with whole neighbourhoods of Protestants around Netherfield Road and Everton Village, as well as throughout other parts of Liverpool. Great Homer Street was generally regarded as the border between the Catholic and Protestant hinterlands in the northern sections of the town.

As a result, the 'Loyal Orange Order' gained significantly in membership numbers and influence. To re-affirm and publicly demonstrate their authority in the town, the 12 July became an annual day of 'Orange Lodge' street decorations, parties, parades, and rallies. On the 'Glorious Twelfth', Liverpool Orangemen regarded it as their God-given right to march with their drum and fife bands, wherever they pleased – including through the Catholic areas of the town. The Irish Catholic communities responded to this with their own marches and demonstrations. Frequently they clashed, and extreme violence and even deaths often resulted.

All the Irish immigrants to Liverpool arrived here through the massive and imposing black gates of Clarence Dock, lying just to the north of the town centre. Opened in 1830, and initially used for steamships, it soon became the harbour for vessels employed on coastal and Irish Sea routes. Therefore these gates were the first sight of Liverpool for the millions of starving, desperate Irish paupers coming here. And yet all that remains to mark this is an inadequately small plaque, mounted high on the outside wall, facing onto the Dock Road. Unveiled at 1.00 p.m., on Sunday, 22 October 2000, it reads (in Gaelic and English): 'Through these gates passed most of the 1,300,000 Liverpool migrants who fled from the Great Famine and 'took the ship' to Liverpool in the years 1845–52 – Remember the Great Famine'.

There is, however, a larger, more appropriate memorial to the victims of the Great Famine, in the gardens of St Luke's Church, on Berry Street.

By the middle of the twentieth century though, the story of the Irish in Liverpool had transformed from one of tragedy to one of triumph; from hostility to harmony; from failure to success. The Irish immigrants, together with all those thousands of people from other lands and cultures who came here, went on to play their part in creating the wonderful character, spirit, and community that is modern Liverpool.

Travelling in overcrowded sailing ships, in desperation and hunger, from Belfast or Dublin to Liverpool could take a long time if the seas were particularly rough or there were storms. Once docked in Liverpool, many ship's captains would tell the uneducated Irish that they were now in New York. The busy streets, with their crowds of people, wagons, horses, omnibuses, tall buildings and warehouses, convinced these poor people that this was indeed so. They had paid for a passage across the Atlantic and, as far as they knew, the Irish Sea was that great ocean. Now they added being swindled and abandoned to their long list of sufferings.

LIVERPOOL WORKHOUSE

The Unhappy Refuge of the Desperate

SO MANY PEOPLE, throughout its long history, have come to Liverpool in the hope of finding a better life. They have either been running away from something, or towards a dream. Sometimes that dream has been realised, but for thousands of people it was not. Some found the the opportunities they needed to change their lives; others did not. In late Georgian and Victorian Liverpool, as in the rest of Britain at that time, when all else failed there was the workhouse.

No one wanted to end up in these parish-run poorhouses, and the people who ran and paid for them did not want people to use them either. The regime they operated was specifically designed to only prevent starvation, not to indulge; to provide the destitute with temporary relief, not permanent residence; to give them work – generally menial tasks – not to supply a permanent job. Life was made deliberately difficult, cold, and sometimes brutal, because inmates were expected to get back out onto the streets and then remain industrious, thrifty, sober, and self-sufficient.

The first workhouse in Liverpool was established, in 1732, at the corner of Hanover Street and College Lane. But this was not large enough to meet the demand: the numbers of the desperate and destitute in the town just seemed to keep growing. And so, in 1772, when the town's population stood at around 20,000 people, a much larger establishment was built; capable of housing up to 600 people – 3 per cent of the population! This was opened on Brownlow Hill; at that time this was out in the country and well outside the built-up area of the town.

The workhouse also contained a prison, or 'House of Correction', as it was officially called. In 1790, this was was described as being 'a vile hole of iniquity'.

In most workhouses in Britain, men were separated from women, mothers from children, and husbands from wives. But at least in the Liverpool Workhouse married couple were sometimes allocated small rooms together – if space and numbers permitted.

Only the most trusted inmates were, very occasionally, allowed to go outside the workhouse, and only then on errands for the staff. This made the whole place like a prison, even for those who were not in the House of Correction. Everyone had to wear a uniform, and they slept in communal dormitories. Whilst they each had a cot or narrow bed, there were no other comforts.

Even the food was very basic, and a weekly menu might consist of:

Breakfast: oatmeal porridge and milk.
Dinner: Monday and Friday, milk pottage and bread; Tuesday, Thursday, Saturday, Scouse (traditional Liverpudlian meat and vegetable stew); Wednesday and Sunday, broth, beef, and bread.
Supper: Monday, Tuesday and Saturday, milk pottage and bread; Wednesday and Sunday, broth, beef, and bread; Thursday and Friday, milk and bread.

This menu was repeated every week, and all food was washed down with either ale or beer, which was far safer to drink than the water.

Many children came into the workhouse as orphans, and were mostly filthy and ridden with lice and nits – or worse – when they arrived. They were cleaned up, fed, and given a rudimentary education. Then, when they were old enough, most of the boys would be sent into the army, whilst the girls would end up in domestic service.

The work that inmates were given depended on their age and gender, and on their degree of health and fitness. Men and able-bodied boys might, if they were

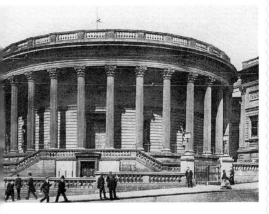

The Picton Library in Liverpool, named after the local architect who described the workhouse building as 'rather cheerful'.

lucky, find themselves working as joiners, blacksmiths, rope-spinners, and cobblers. Women and girls would be expected to weave baskets and bonnets, knit stockings, sew, stitch clothes, or weave basic garments. For those less able, or when the workhouse staff were less than kind, the work could be bottle-washing – hot, heavy, dangerous, and repetitive.

But again, this was part of the 'reformatory' purpose of the workhouse. The daily timetable was:

6.00:	Rise
6.30-7.00:	Breakfast
7.00-12.00:	Work
12.00-13.00:	Dinner
13.00-18.00:	Work
18.00-19.00:	Supper
20.00:	Bedtime

Sunday was a day of rest and, during the winter, inmates were allowed to get up an hour later and did not start work until 8.00 a.m.

No one escaped work unless they were desperately ill, not even the infirm and elderly. The work that was generally reserved for these people was picking oakum.

Oakum was the loose fibres of rope, blended together with tar, and sold to ship-builders or the navy. It was used as 'caulking' to seal the hulls of wooden sailing vessels. But creating it was a tedious and unpleasant task, common in Victorian workhouses and prisons, including those in Liverpool. Workers were given lengths of old rope, the many twisted strands of which they had to unpick, unwind, and separate. This was very hard work, and it was painful: it chafed skin and tore fingernails.

Infringements of the rules called for strict discipline, which was often administered with real enthusiasm by the staff.

For minor offences, such as swearing or pretending to be ill to get out of work, inmates would be fed on only bread and

In 1823, three remarkably long-lived residents of the Liverpool Workhouse died: Ellen Tate, aged 110; Francis Dixon, aged 105; and Margaret McKenzie, aged 104. So perhaps things were not always bad behind those dark, high walls!

water for two days – even children. For more serious offences, such as refusing or resisting orders, answering back or 'cheeking', or for fighting, inmates could be locked in a cell for a number of days, again fed only on bread and water. For really serious offences the courts or the police might be brought in, and the full might of Victorian justice would fall on the offender.

Children under fourteen years of age would be flogged, and so could adults too. In the courtyard stood a whipping post, at which the female inmates could be lashed. A water pump in the men's yard was used for similar purposes. There was also a 'cuckstool' or ducking chair, suspended over a deep tub of water; this was used 'to bring refractory prisoners to their senses'.

However, by the mid-nineteenth century, and under the stewardship of Mrs Widdows, conditions for all prisoners – male and female – had significantly improved. She had drastically reduced the number of whippings, had done away with the cuckstool, and ensured that the inmates had a daily allowance of a two-penny loaf, two pounds of potatoes, and a measure of salt.

By 1846, despite various additions, the Brownlow Hill Workhouse was generally acknowledged to be inadequate and, over the next ten to twelve years, it was gradually demolished and rebuilt. The local architect, Sir James Picton, described the new institution by saying, 'its general aspect is anything but repulsive.... it has a rather cheerful and pleasant outlook', but the perspective was different if you were an inmate, within its very high and all-surrounding walls.

There were twenty-six buildings in the rebuilt institution, including dormitories for inmates, a laundry, stables, a dining hall (with seating for 1,000), a bakery, a butcher's shop, shoemaker's and tailors' workshops, a medical block, a mortuary, a chapel, and a home for the nurses and staff. The workhouse also had its own graveyard, outside the walls but very close, and this was in regular use.

The Governor, however, lived in a separate house in the site, which had five bedrooms, accommodation and facilities for servants (who were workhouse inmates), and a large store for wine under the stairs.

This was the largest workhouse in England, and one of the largest in Europe. It covered 9 acres of land, and had been built to accommodate up to 3,000 people, of all ages. However, at its peak, towards the end of the nineteenth century, up to 5,000 people were crammed inside its intimidating perimeter, often sleeping six to a bed. Most of these were Irish Roman Catholics, who had come to Liverpool escaping poverty and starvation – only to find themselves no better off. But even life in the workhouse was better that dying in the streets of starvation or cholera.

The Liverpool Workhouse survived until 1928, when the revision of the Poor Laws closed it and brought the property onto the market. It entire site was sold, on 26 March 1930, to the Roman Catholic Archdiocese, and all the buildings were demolished.

The Metropolitan Cathedral of Christ the King now stands on the site of what was once a place of desperation and humiliation.

AD 1832

THE BLACK SPOT ON THE MERSEY

IN THE EIGHTEENTH and early nineteenth centuries, and in common with every other town and city in Britain, Liverpool and its people stank.

There was little water for washing, and this was not a priority anyway. Indeed, few people bathed as, particularly amongst the lower classes, this was actually considered to be unhealthy.

This meant that clothes were seldom washed either, adding to the general offensiveness of the people. As a result, those men and women who were working, and especially in the manufacturing industries of the times, were almost impregnated with the smells of their workplaces. Those who worked in the slaughterhouse, or as butchers, always smelled of meat and blood. The sugar workers always smelt of sugar; ropeworkers always smelled of rope and tar; sailmakers of canvas; and those that worked in the tanneries – one of the most unpleasant environments – smelt particularly vile, especially as one of the ingredients used in the tanning process was rotten pigs' flesh.

Whenever the wealthier people ventured in the poorer or more densely populated areas, especially amongst 'the common people', they would carry posies of flowers, or 'nosegays', to clutch by their noses. This was not only a way of masking the smell of the people and the town, but was seen as a protection against 'bad air', which they believed could infect them with illness or disease: they were not entirely wrong in this, of course.

The streets were awash with horse manure too, as these animals provided the motive power for all forms of commercial and public transport.

Whilst the successful ship-owners, slave-traders, mill and factory proprietors, merchants, and entrepreneurs became ever more wealthy, powerful, and comfortable, those ordinary people of Liverpool who had generated that wealth were trapped in their poverty. The wealthier classes wanted to move out of the smells and crowds of the town to the more rural outlying districts: these would eventually become the suburban areas of Liverpool, like Crosby, Woolton, Allerton, and Childwall. They left their large Georgian town houses behind them in the town centre.

Possibly renting them out themselves for extra income, or selling them to opportunistic landlords, these large properties, with their many rooms, attics, and cellars, were now left to the poor and the working classes. Often with more than one family in every room, these people were paying rent for what rapidly degenerated into extremely filthy and overcrowded accommodation. After the upper floors had been filled with new tenants, the cellars soon filled up too, and these properties rapidly became Liverpool's first slums.

In 1841, there were over 6,000 cellars in Liverpool, in which more than 22,000 people lived. Liverpool, in fact, had more cellar dwellings than any other town in England. Most of these would only be 10ft or 12ft square, and the ceilings were often so low that adults could not always stand fully upright. These places could also be home to more than one family, and up to thirty people could be found living in a single cellar.

Because Liverpool is on the coast, and has many watercourses running across and beneath it, dampness was widespread in these cellars. In fact, in the Whitechapel and Paradise Street areas, and also in houses built on the land reclaimed from the former Pool, flooding was a common occurrence. The consequences for those people living in these subterranean spaces must have been atrocious. Because human and animal waste was largely piled up in middens in the streets or alleyways, or was filling up cess-pits. When there were heavy rains or flooding, all of this excrement would be washed around the streets, or ooze into the very homes of the people – and especially into the cellar dwellings.

It was around this time too that a more notorious form of accommodation was created by private speculators and landlords – the court dwelling. These comprised a central square, about 20-30ft long by about 10-15ft wide, around which blocks of rooms had been built, often up to four floors high. Each block accommodated dozens of families, and again there could often be more than one family in each room.

Court dwellings were accessed by a narrow gate or passageway that, from the outside at least, might have looked like a normal doorway or entry in the front of a terrace of houses. However, these would lead directly into the courtyard and the self-contained complex of tenemented rooms. Even before the creation of Liverpool's first dock, there were already many such court dwellings in the town.

These confined urban communities would not have had any form of localised water supply, and the only sanitary provision for the hundreds of people living around each court might have been a single, communal water-closet, placed at one end of the yard. These would generally consist of a wooden bench with a lavatory hole cut in it, suspended over an earth pit. Sometimes there might be a full or half door on these cubicles, and sometimes not; but, in such dense filth and poverty, a lack of personal privacy was a minor consideration.

If not flowing into cess-pits, or scooped out to be added to the public middens, the contents of these lavatories would be emptied by the 'night-soil' men, but not always on a regular or predictable basis. Tenants would have to pay for this service in addition to their basic rent. If they could not afford this, then the filth simply accumulated and overflowed.

As far as the underprivileged of Liverpool were concerned, only two things sustained them: a developing sense of shared suffering, and therefore solidarity-of-community, and a hope and faith in the afterlife to come. In fact, religious faith was often the only solace for many Liverpudlians, at what was soon to be a time of yet more social transformation and upheaval, as Britain became increasingly industrialised and class-structured.

During the eighteenth and nineteenth centuries, most deaths in the town were caused by endemic diseases such as tuberculosis, typhus, typhoid, occasional

Open-air tuberculosis wards in Liverpool. (Courtesy of the Library of Congress, Prints & Photographs Division, LC-USZ62-124112)

epidemics of cholera, and especially by diseases of childhood, including diarrhoea, dysentery, diphtheria, measles, whooping cough, and scarlet fever.

Between 1780 and 1796, around 40,000 people were stricken with typhus, which was spread by lice or fleas carried in the clothing as well as on the bodies of people. Following chills, delirium, and stupor, the next symptoms were severe pain in the joints and muscles, dreadful headaches, and a red rash all over the body that wept blood. Victims could be dead within two weeks.

Bedbugs, although not carrying infection themselves, could spread disease. When people scratched their bites with unwashed hands, in unhygienic surrounding, germs from the insect's faeces would embed themselves into the wounds, which then became infected. In the days before penicillin and other antibiotics, such infections themselves frequently proved fatal.

Then cholera struck the town. This is a water-borne disease that causes watery diarrhoea, vomiting, and very painful muscle cramps. These symptoms can develop within one or two days of someone being infected. In severe cases, it is possible for a person to experience more serious symptoms, such as a rapid loss of body fluids, which can lead to dehydration, shock, and a painful death.

In 1823, a cholera epidemic took the lives of more than 1,500 Liverpudlians and infected a further 5,000. In 1832, another cholera epidemic killed 1,523 people. Many people fled the town, but those that were forced to stay were angry that the Corporation seemed to be taking no action. There were a series of disturbances in Liverpool. Crowds attacked doctors and hospitals, and the newspapers called these disturbances 'the Cholera Riots'. The year 1849 saw another major cholera epidemic that killed 5,308; in 1854, another outbreak killed 1,290 people.

Child mortality in Liverpool, during the mid-nineteenth century in particular, was amongst the highest in Britain. In 1832, a local doctor reported that less than a third of the children of the town lived beyond the age of two. In fact, conditions were so poor that only half of Liverpool's children lived beyond the age of ten.

However, the Corporation of Liverpool began to attempt to tackle these problems and, on the 1 January 1847, they appointed the world's first medical officer of health, Dr William Henry Duncan (1805–1863). Doctor Duncan himself named his town 'the Black Spot on the Mersey', and described it as 'the most unhealthy town in England.'

The average life-expectancy in the poorest districts of the town was seventeen years of age. By comparison, and at the same time, life expectancy in similar districts of Manchester was twenty, and in London poor people might expect to live to the age of twenty-six. Over half of every 1,000 deaths in Victorian Liverpool were of children under the age of five, and in the Irish Catholic areas of the town – the most densely populated – the death rate was 50 people in every 1,000.

Duncan recognised that there was a clear link between housing conditions and the outbreak of diseases, such as cholera, small-pox, and typhus, and he worked closely with the borough engineer, James Newlands (1813–1871), also recently appointed.

Together, these dedicated and skilled men, and their staff, began to tackle the problems of poor housing and sanitary provision in the town. They encouraged the Corporation to clear away the cramped, unsavoury slum-dwellings, and to replace them with spacious and well-ventilated new housing: Britain's first Council Housing.

Slowly but surely, living conditions for ordinary people in Liverpool began to improve.

AD 1864

THE 'BIG BANG' ON THE MERSEY

Eleven Tons of Gunpowder and the Clap Of Doom

NEAR VALE PARK in New Brighton, on the Wirral Peninsular, stands a castellated gateway. Proudly dominating the corner of Magazine Lane and Magazine Brow, this once gave entrance to the Liscard Battery. This small fortress was built in 1858, armed with cannon, and provided with accommodation for regular soldiers. Part of a system of fortifications, constructed on both sides of the river, the Battery was built as a defence against any potential invaders, especially after our battles with the French during the Napoleonic Wars.

Opposite the battery, on the other side of Fort Street, were Liscard Magazines (hence the local street names). It was here, from 1768 until 1851, that ships were required to deposit their supplies of gunpowder whilst visiting Liverpool. After this time though, and because of many complaints about the threat of explosion, special vessels anchored off New Ferry were used for this purpose, so posing less of a risk to local people.

However, these safety precautions were useless when munitions ships were sailing into or out of the River Mersey. And such was the case of the small merchant ship, the *Lottie Sleigh*.

On 15 January 1864, this three-masted, wooden sailing barque, built in 1852, had just taken on a consignment of gunpowder – 11 tons of it, to be precise. She was anchored in the middle of the Mersey, midway between Liverpool and its sister towns of Birkenhead and Wallasey, on the Wirral, and was preparing to sail. However, whilst most of the crew were on deck making ready, a steward down below was trimming a paraffin lamp.

A slight swell was on the river and a wave caught the ship, rocking her. This threw the steward off balance and he tipped the lamp over, spilling oil. He made to grab the lamp, but accidently ignited the oil with the lighted taper he was holding instead. The paraffin burst into flames and began to spread across the lower deck: very quickly the wooden walls were ablaze too.

The steward raced up on deck, calling out the alarm as he ran, literally, for his life. The crew all realised that they only had a matter of minutes before the fire reached the hold – and its massive cargo of gunpowder. So, to a man, the crew jumped overboard – the captain too, so there would be no 'going down with the ship' that day. Everyone began to swim as fast and as far away as they could, from what was now a floating time-bomb on a very short fuse.

Above Entrance gates to the old Liscard Battery.

Right Vale Park, New Brighton, near to the Battery. The munitions were eventually moved from this area onto ships, but they proved no safer: the sound of the Lottie Sleigh *exploding could be heard from here – and indeed, from up to 4 miles away.*

Above The approach to Rock Ferry – sailing from this port, the Wasp *spotted the blazing* Lottie Sleigh.

But then, and not realising that *Lottie Sleigh* was a munitions ship, the captain of the steam ferryboat *Wasp*, sailing from Rock Ferry to Liverpool, saw the flames aboard the barque and the men in the water. He immediately made speed towards them to pick them all up. This man was a genuine hero – even though the first men his boat rescued instantly warned him about the danger, the *Wasp* stayed until it had saved every crew member; only then did it steam, at full speed, away from the blazing ship.

Then *Lottie Sleigh* blew up.

The sound of the explosion was ear-splitting, and was described at the time as being 'like a hundred thunderbolts rolled together', and 'as the clap of doom heralding the world's end'. The noise carried for 30 miles, as far away as Chester, from where the authorities immediately sent a telegraph message to Liverpool asking urgently what had caused the incredible bang! But it was the terrific blast of air that did the real damage, and a report at the time said:

Its effects in every part of Liverpool were severely felt and created indescribable terror. At the same time the most solid blocks of warehouses, offices and private dwellings were shaken to their base – doors locked and bolted were thrown wide open – hundreds, yea even thousands of squares of glass were smashed.

Most of the gas lamps in Liverpool were blown out. People were knocked off their feet, and ships tethered at the quaysides in the docks were set rocking and straining at their moorings.

Almost every pane of glass in the buildings facing the Wirral side of the river were also shattered, and many buildings were damaged there as well.

Eventually, when all had quietened down and Merseysiders had recovered from their shock and terror, and when all the smoke had cleared, the burning wreckage from the *Lottie Sleigh* could be seen floating down the river. This sad hulk was eventually towed to New Ferry, where it was beached and later broken up.

All that survived of the ship was the large figurehead, carved in the form of a well-proportioned woman – perhaps 'Lottie' herself? This was virtually unscathed and her painted colours remained bright. She has blond hair and blue eyes, and is dressed in a crinoline dress of black, blue, and white. She can now be seen in Liverpool's Maritime Museum, staring off into the distance; a silent reminder of an exceptionally noisy event.

Shrapnel from the explosion aboard the *Lottie Sleigh* travelled over 4 miles, splitting some of the branches of the 1,000 year-old Allerton Oak Tree, out at Calderstones. This is why, even today, some of its great limbs are still supported by large iron rods, put there after the explosion to repair the damage.

Fortunately, the old tree still thrives, and produces an annual crop of acorns.

AD 1837–1920

SPRING-HEELED JACK

The Malevolent Sprite of Everton

FOR MOST OF the nineteenth and well into the twentieth centuries, a bizarre, leaping character was being reported all over England, terrorising – and occasionally attacking – innocent bystanders.

Between 1837 and 1920, a total of eighty-three years, sightings of this bizarre character were reported, mainly in London, but also all over Britain, including Liverpool – in the districts of Toxteth, Aigburth, Childwall, and twice in Everton. Described as a tall, thin, powerful man, wearing a black cloak, 'Spring-Heeled Jack', as he became known, had large, pointed ears, an equally sharp nose and hands like skeletal claws. He also had red glowing eyes, which seemed to protrude from his face, and he could spit white and blue flames from his mouth.

Most remarkable of all, though, was that he was able to jump 20-30ft vertically, and 'leap tall buildings at a single bound'. Jack made a habit of terrorising people, especially women, by appearing suddenly and then noisily spouting his flames at them. He would then spring away again, just as abruptly.

There are many detailed reports of incidents involving Jack, some given by vicars,

policemen, and other such pillars of the community. The first definite evidence of his existence comes from London, where complaints became so numerous about the amazing 'Jumping Man' that the Lord Mayor instructed the police to investigate a series of mysterious appearances and attacks, apparently all perpetrated by Jack.

One such incident was reported to local magistrates, in 1837, by a Miss Jane Alsop. She was twenty-five years old, and lived with her father and two sisters in an isolated house near Bow. She reported that, 'just before 9 o'clock at night, there came a violent ringing at the front-gate bell', which Jane answered herself. At her door she saw a tall man, whom she described as being 'wrapped head to toe in a black cloak'.

'For God's sake give me a light,' the man gasped out, in a gruff and breathless voice. Then she added, 'For we have caught Spring-Heeled Jack in the lane!'

The young woman immediately fetched a candle and handed it to the stranger. No sooner had she done so, than he threw back his cloak and hissed loudly at her. What Jane saw terrified her: the man's body was encased in 'some kind of white oilskin, close fitting him entirely', and he was 'a creature

The steeple where the famous Spring-Heeled Jack, above, was seen. (Engraving with kind permission of Neil R. Storey.)

of hideous and frightful aspect'! On his head was a helmet, below which his eyes 'glowed like red fireballs'.

Suddenly, this grotesque figure leapt upon the defenceless Jane, spurting blue and white flames from his mouth, and clawing at her dress and body with sharp, metallic claws. Her screams drew her sisters to her aid and, as they arrived at the scene, the terrifying figure bounded away into the distance, 'making great leaping strides' as he did so.

The story of this attack was given more credibility when, a few days later, the same magistrates received a report from a young man named Scales. Two nights before the attack on Jane Alsop, he had discovered his two sisters being attacked in the lane near his home in Limehouse. His independent description of the attacker, corroborated by his sisters, was the same as that given by Jane.

In 1843, Spring-Heeled Jack appeared in Northamptonshire, Hampshire, and East Anglia, where he frightened the drivers of mail coaches. Two years later he was seen in West London.

Throughout the 1850s and 1860s, Spring-Heeled Jack stories sprung up (rather like him) all over the country, with appearances being reported as far afield as Warwickshire, Staffordshire, Lincolnshire, Worcestershire, Middlesex, and Surrey. By the 1870s he was back, terrorising parts of London once more. Indeed, in 1888, it was once believed that Spring-

---

Possibly the first appearance of Spring-Heeled Jack was near Clapham in London, in October 1837. In broad daylight, eye-witnesses reported that he jumped in front of a coach, terrifying the horses and the coachman. The animals bolted and the driver lost control, crashing his coach and sustaining severe injuries. Jack simply jumped over a nearby high fence, chattering to himself and squealing with laughter.

Heeled Jack might also have been Jack the Ripper, as he had been sighted making his fire-spitting leaps in and around the area of the Whitechapel murders. But then he came to Liverpool.

He was first seen in the early 1880s, in Toxteth, scurrying up High Park Street. He disappeared down passageways and entries, only to suddenly reappear again by leaping over the houses. Then, as quickly as he had arrived, he bounded off towards the river.

A few years later he was back in Liverpool again, this time jumping over garden walls in the quiet, suburban community of St Michaels-in-the-Hamlet, near Aigburth. He was also seen leaping around All Saints' church and the Childwall Abbey Inn, in Childwall. Then Jack made his first appearance in Everton, in 1888, jumping over houses and spitting his flames at people all around Shaw Street. The final time that Spring-Heeled Jack was publicly reported in Liverpool was in 1904, and it was in exactly the same area of Everton.

In broad daylight, he was first spotted in the district hanging from the steeple of St Francis Xavier's church, on Salisbury Street. Hundreds of onlookers claimed that he then suddenly dropped from the steeple and fell to the ground. Thinking that he had committed suicide, they rushed to the point where he had landed – behind some houses – only to find a helmeted man, clothed in white, standing there waiting for them.

As soon as the crowd appeared, he scuttled towards them, raised his arms, spread his bat-like cape, spat flame, and snarled. Then, abruptly, he took to the air over William Henry Street, leaping in gigantic bounds, up and down from roadway to rooftop and back to the ground again.

This extraordinary bouncing spectacle continued for about ten or twelve minutes before Jack simply disappeared. Many people were subsequently willing to confirm publicly what they had seen, including police officers and priests. However, from that day to this all sightings of Spring-Heeled Jack ceased – unless people are just not prepared to admit they have seen him!

Several theories have been proposed to attempt to explain this phenomenon, including: a normal man with some sort of spring apparatus on his feet; an insane fire-eater; a costumed acrobat; a malicious phantom; or even the Devil himself! Indeed, it was reported that cloven footprints had been found at the site of one of the incidents. But nothing explains how the same creature could continue to surprise, outrage, and terrify Britain for over eighty years.

Nor has anything conclusively explained who or what he actually was. But mums and dads around Everton, wanting to quieten unruly or noisy children, will still say, 'If you don't behave, Spring-Heeled Jack will get you!'

AD 1912

THE *TITANIC* TRAGEDY

Unsinkable Arrogance and Icy Death

RMS *TITANIC* WAS the second of three Olympic-sized liners designed and built at the Harland and Wolff shipyard in Belfast, between 1908 and 1914. When she was launched, in May 1911, she was the largest ship afloat – standing as high as an eleven-storey building. *Titanic* was owned by the White Star Line, who had their headquarters in Liverpool, in Albion House, which still stands on the corner of James Street and the Strand.

However, during the design stage the White Star Line decided that not only would extra lifeboats clutter up the decks, but that they could save a great deal of money by having only a minimal number on board. This view was endorsed by the British Board of Trade, which confirmed that twenty lifeboats, with a capacity of 1,178 places, was perfectly acceptable.

The ship's owners were so confident of the sophistication and technological excellence of their design, and in the quality of her construction, that they proudly promoted and advertised *Titanic* as being 'unsinkable', even though the vessel's chief designer had never made such a claim himself. The arrogance of that statement was to come back and haunt everyone connected with the great liner.

White Star Offices, now Albion house, a few years before the tragedy.

On 10 April 1912, she set sail with over 2,229 passengers and crew on board, on her maiden voyage from Southampton to New York, via Queenstown in Southern Ireland. The journey was smooth and they were making good time. Then, at 11.40 p.m. on the night of 14 April 1912, just off Cape Race in the North Atlantic, and with the ocean 'almost as still as a mill pond', everything changed.

The lookout in the crow's nest was the first to spot something in the water, right in front of the ship. He was Fred Fleet, from Liverpool, and he soon saw that the object was a great iceberg, even though he had not been issued with binoculars. Fred survived the ensuing disaster, and at the inquiry, he said that: 'It was a dark night as well, with no moonlight... And the lookouts had no binoculars; the only pair was left back at Southampton.'

This meant that he had hardly any time at all to issue a warning. But Fleet immediately rang the warning bell in the lookout station, and phoned down to the bridge.

Frederick Fleet. (Courtesy of the Library of Congress, Prints & Photographs Division, LC-DIG-hec-00939)

'What did you see?' asked duty officer.

'Iceberg, right ahead!' he replied.

The officer simply said, 'Thank you,' and put down the receiver.

On the bridge the order was given, 'Hard astarboard'! At the same time, the ship's telegraph, to the engine room, was first set to 'All Stop', and then to 'All Reverse Full'. The ship's wheel was now over as far as it would go, as everyone on the bridge strained to see forward in the darkness, and as the giant iceberg loomed into view. It struck the side of the vessel and gouged a great gash right along her side, below the water line – and from that moment on, the unsinkable *Titanic* was a doomed vessel.

The captain, Edward Smith (born 1850), who had lived in Liverpool for forty years, had been asleep in his cabin when the message was phoned through to him, and he immediately made his way to the bridge.

'What have we struck?' He asked, 'An iceberg, sir,' came the reply. Smith immediately ordered a damage inspection. He received the report within 20 minutes, and was left in no doubt that he was now the captain of a stricken ship, which was slowly, but inevitably, sinking into the freezing waters of the North Atlantic Ocean.

Even though it was likely that the ship had been travelling too fast to avoid the iceberg, the vessel actually took so long to go down that everybody could have survived – if there had been sufficient lifeboats. And even though all the lifeboats on board were successfully launched as the vessel began to settle in the water, this staggering lack of capacity meant that only 713 people were rescued. Perhaps predictably, considering the class-ridden culture of the time, there were more first-class male survivors in the boats than third-class children.

Titanic's death was a protracted one, and the great ship did not finally disappear below the waves, with the loss of 1,516 lives, until 2.20 a.m. on the morning of Monday 15 April.

Two years after the *Titanic* disaster, but overshadowed by her story, another Liverpool registered liner went down at sea. Largely forgotten now, the *Empress of Ireland* was sailing in thick fog, in the St Lawrence River in Canada, when the Norwegian collier *Storstad* collided with her. This was at around 2.30 a.m., on 29 May 1914, and most of her 1,054 passengers and 413 crew were asleep.

The liner only took 15 minutes to sink, and 840 passengers lost their lives: 172 members of the crew died too, most of them from Liverpool.

There had been enough life-jackets for all 2,229 people on board, and almost everyone was wearing one, so many more people could have been saved if they had been able get into lifeboats, or if a rescue ship had come sooner than it did. In fact, there was only one vessel that arrived in time to pick up survivors: the Liverpool-registered *Carpathia*. However, this did not arrive until 4.00 a.m. It rescued all 713 survivors from the lifeboats – but there could have been more. One of the first of these to leave *Titanic* carried only twenty-eight people, though it could have held sixty-four. In all, there were 472 lifeboat seats not used.

Very few people actually went down with the ship. Of those passengers and crew who could not get aboard a lifeboat, yet managed to get into the sea safely, almost all perished because the waters of the North Atlantic were so intolerably cold. The temperature of the Atlantic that night was 31 degrees, which rapidly drained their energies and sapped their will to live. 'The sound of people drowning,' said survivor Ms Eva Hart, 'is something I cannot describe to you – and neither can anyone else. It's the most dreadful sound – and there's a dreadful silence that follows it.'

When the rescue vessels did eventually arrive, it was far too late to save the men, women, and children who had escaped into the water, and all they found were 330 frozen corpses, wearing life-belts, bobbing about in the calm but icy waters. Many other floating bodies were not found because they had drifted off.

Amongst the crew aboard *Titanic*, roughly 10 per cent were from Liverpool, or had some connection with the city, and many families here lost relatives that

Two tiny survivors: this photograph, part of the George Bain collection, shows Michel and Edmond Navratil (aged four and two) after they were rescued from the disaster. Their French father died aboard the Titanic. *(Courtesy of the Library of Congress, Prints & Photographs Division, LC-DIG-ggbain-10354*

The Titanic Memorial at Princes Dock.

Even today the magnitude of this disaster resonates clearly, particularly as it was so completely avoidable.

There are two memorials to the *Titanic* disaster in Liverpool, and one of these is at the Pier Head, between the Liver Building and Princes Dock. This is an obelisk, built as a result of the sinking, and erected following a public subscription. It was unveiled in 1916, and was originally intended to be a memorial to the thirty-two engineers who stayed at their posts aboard *Titanic* on that fateful night.

None of the engineers or engineering officers survived from the ship; they stayed at their posts almost until the great vessel sank beneath the Atlantic, keeping the boilers stoked and fired, and the ship's lights burning, in the vain hope of attracting rescue ships in time to save everybody aboard.

The First World War broke out before the monument was completed and so its dedication was broadened: it now commemorates all ships' engineers and stokers who have lost their lives at sea. As such, it is officially called the 'Memorial to the Engine Room Heroes'. However, it will always be known locally as 'The *Titanic* Memorial', and it attracts much attention because of this association.

Its inscription reads:

'The brave do not die,
their deeds live for ever and call upon us
to emulate their courage and devotion to
duty.'

dreadful night. In fact, so many of the crew came from the Vauxhall area of Liverpool that the main gangway in the crew quarters aboard the ship was known as 'Scotland Road', which runs through one of Liverpool's most highly-populated districts. Most crew members, however, came from our sister seafaring town of Southampton. Of these, 637 people died, completely devastating the community there.

The second memorial to the *Titanic* disaster is dedicated to the ship's band. This can be found in the foyer of the Philharmonic Hall on Hope Street, and it lists the names of all the musicians who continued to play as the ship began to sink. Their final melody was not 'Nearer My God To Thee', as many people believe, but 'Songe d'Automne.

AD 1914–1918

THE LIVERPOOL PALS

Mud, Blood and Death in the Trenches

IVERPOOL HAS, FOR genera-tions, provided soldiers for the British Army, so much so that the renowned King's Regiment has always been made up mainly of Liverpool men – and such was the case on the declaration of the First World War (1914–1918).

In Britain, in 1914, the outbreak of the conflict was a time of romantic patri-otism and imperialist jingoism: posters appeared everywhere of Lord Kitchener (1850–1916), who was Secretary of State for War. He was shown, behind his great moustache, pointing his finger and stat-ing 'Britain Needs You': prompting the young men of Britain to see themselves as the nation's saviours and heroes. This was a time too when old soldiers from previ-ous imperial wars were also urging young men, especially in Liverpool, to 'get out there and see some action'; 'if you don't go now,' they said, 'you'll miss it. It'll all be over by Christmas!' These youngsters – for such they were – could not even escape the propaganda in the music halls, because their favourite female singers would regale them with rousing choruses of, 'We don't want to lose you but we think you ought to go'. Girlfriends and fiancées also told their young men that they should

go to war, and 'do their bit for King and Country'.

What was a young man to do? He would receive a white feather in the post if he did not sign up, marking him out as a coward. Many more men actively wanted to go, to sign up for a grand adventure. So, go they did; in their thousands. But an adventure was the last thing this war was going to be, because of the complete failure, on the part of the country's military and political lead-ers, to recognise the implications of fighting a modern, mechanised war. No one had any conception of the unprecedented horrors that this was about to unleash on an unsus-pecting Europe. And so Liverpool's young men went to fight in the muddy swamps that were the trenches of France and Bel-gium – and they went as 'Pals'.

It was Edward George Villiers Stanley (1865–1948), the 17th Earl of Derby, whose idea it was to recruit groups of young men who were already comrades and friends, to form a new fighting regiment. An advert appeared in the local newspapers, on 27 August 1914, suggesting that men wishing to join 'a battalion of comrades, to serve their country together' should report to the headquarters of the 5th Battalion, the King's Liverpool Regiment.

King George inspecting the docks at Liverpool during the First World War. (Courtesy of the Library of Congress, Prints & Photographs Division, LC-DIG-ggbain-24632)

Kitchener says, 'More men, and still more men, till the enemy is crushed!' (Courtesy of the Library of Congress, Prints & Photographs Division LC-USZC4-10883)

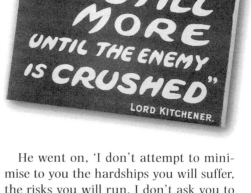

The sheer number of men who turned up overwhelmed the recruiting hall, and extra rooms had to be opened to deal with the numbers who wanted to enlist; already there were enough to form two battalions. They were then all told to come to St George's Hall, on 31 August, where they would be officially enlisted. Here, Lord Derby took the opportunity to deliver a rousing, patriotic speech to an audience of 1,050 new recruits, using the phrase 'Liverpool Pals' for the first time. 'This should be a Battalion of Pals,' the 17th Earl told them, 'a battalion in which friends from the same office will fight shoulder to shoulder for the honour of Britain and the credit of Liverpool.'

He went on, 'I don't attempt to minimise to you the hardships you will suffer, the risks you will run. I don't ask you to uphold Liverpool's honour; it would be an insult to think that you could do anything but that. But I do thank you from the bottom of my heart for coming here tonight, and showing what is the spirit of Liverpool – a spirit that ought to spread through every city and every town in the kingdom.'

And they continued to sign up; men and boys from all over Liverpool. They did so in small groups, as 'mates'; as complete neighbourhood football teams; as bands of apprentices or workers from single factories, offices, and shipping lines; as neighbours from single streets; as fellow worshippers in churches; and as gangs of lads from corner pubs. The response to the emotional recruitment campaigns was phenomenal, so much so that the volunteers eventually made up four battalions of the King's Regiment Liverpool: the 17th, 18th, 19th and 20th; each regiment comprising an average of 1,400 men.

The Wirral Battalion of the Cheshire Regiment was equally significant, with young men from all over the towns and villages of the Peninsular leaving their homes and loved ones to fight overseas. The largest contingent of these recruits joined from Port Sunlight, mainly from the Lever Brother's Works. Indeed, the greatest number of volunteers obtained from any works in the country came from this Wirral soap factory.

In late 1915, the Liverpool Pals battalions were sent to training camps in France, near the River Somme, ready for what was being called 'The Big Push' in the summer of the following year. And, on the morning of 1 July 1916, the Liverpool Pals were on the front line.

Then the order came, and these young Liverpudlians went 'over the top' into No Man's Land: almost 200 of them were immediately killed, and over 300 more were either wounded, taken prisoner, or declared missing. Most of those who died in the mud and the blood of that dreadful battlefield never had their own graves. These soldiers are remembered on the Memorial to the Missing of the Somme, at Thiepval in France.

Of the four original Pals Battalions who sailed to France in November 1915, 20 per cent would be dead by the end of

Miles and miles of trenches, stretching into the distance.

the war. If the figures of the wounded are added to this, the actual number of casualties is nearer 75 per cent. These young men died and suffered as proud Liverpudlians, determined to do their duty as they saw it.

Writing home to his family on the eve of his regiment's departure for France, and destined to be killed, one young soldier, Private W.B. Owens, wrote;

> Well, we're away at last, and 'tho no one feels that it's a solemn occasion to be in England for perhaps the last time, I think that the predominant feeling in every chap's heart – in mine, at any rate – is one of pride and great content at being chosen to fight and endure for our dear ones and the old country.

Many young men from all over Merseyside lied about their ages to join up, often with the collusion and encouragement of family, friends, and of the Recruiting Sergeants. Boys as young as fourteen went overseas – flushed with pride – to end their young lives in the mud and the filth. Thousands more were gassed, mutilated, wounded, and psychologically damaged, but at least they were alive.

However, thousands of the Liverpool Pals and the Wirral Battalion were not, and they were among the 13,000 Liverpool and Wirral soldiers who were massacred on the European battlefronts, and in the trenches of that foreign field 'that is forever England'.

During the First World War – the 'war to end all wars' – 5,397,000 men were mobilised. Of these, 703,000 were killed and 1,663,000 wounded. This is a total of 2,367,000 war casualties, or 44 per cent of the serving men.

One of the heroes of the conflict, though, was Noel Godfrey Chavasse from Liverpool. He received the Victoria Cross twice – one of only three people so honoured – for saving the lives of his comrades on the battlefield. Tragically, Noel too was killed. His medals were awarded posthumously.

HITLER'S ORDER – 'OBLITERATE LIVERPOOL!'

The May Blitz of 1941

LIVERPOOL'S ROLE THROUGH-OUT the Second World War cannot be underestimated, particularly because this was the place from where the Battle of the Atlantic was fought.

This was the campaign to defend the North Atlantic Convoys which, throughout the war, brought vital supplies to Liverpool, and from here to the rest of the country. Sailing into the Mersey from the Western Approaches, they came here from America, Russia, and countries of the British Empire. The convoys were protected by British warships because Hitler sent his submarine fleets – the U-Boat hunter-killer packs – to wipe out these merchant vessels.

When war was declared, in September 1939, the 'Operational Headquarters for Atlantic Defence and Conflict' were being constructed in the basement of Derby House, under Exchange Flags at the rear of the Town Hall. Upon completion, in 1941, this became the home of the Western Approaches Command, known as 'The Citadel'. It was from here that the Battle of the Atlantic was fought, from 50,000 square ft of gas-proof and bomb-proof bunkers, beneath Liverpool.

Here, deep underground in over 100 rooms – and with the most sophisticated communications and code-breaking equipment available – the Battle of the Atlantic was fought. This included the sinking of the German Battleship *Bismarck*, amongst many other enemy vessels.

The first attack on a British ship was the sinking of the SS *Athenia*, which was on its way from Liverpool to Canada, only 24 hours after the outbreak of the conflict. The final encounter of this campaign was the sinking of the British freighter *Avondale Park*, and of a Norwegian minesweeper, in the final days of the war, in May 1945.

Atlantic convoys were always protected by an escort force, commanded by the well-respected Captain Frederick John 'Johnnie' Walker (1896–1944), whose leadership skills were renowned. His tactics were very successful, and on just one patrol in March 1944, his officers and men sank six German U-Boats.

During the Battle of the Atlantic, the Allied shipping losses were astronomical. Over 12.8 million tons of Allied and neutral shipping was destroyed, but the loss of life was the real catastrophe: Royal Naval losses totalled 73,600; plus 30,248 killed from the Merchant Service; 6,000 from Coastal Command; and 29,000 from the Anti-U-Boat Flotilla. Memorials to these

U-Boat attack! Liverpool's shipping faced great peril during the war.

sustained raids on any part of Britain, including London, and was an all-or-nothing attempt by the Germans to wreck the port from which the Western Approaches were being defended. After this, the Nazis continued to bomb the city almost every night, during the remainder of May and through the first two weeks of June.

Altogether, there were seventy-nine separate air raids during the Blitz. It was estimated that, out of the almost 300,000 homes in Liverpool at that time, around 200,000 were damaged – 11,000 of those being destroyed. Indeed, throughout the city and its suburbs, there were 15,000 Blitzed sites.

The centre of the city lay in waste, and the entire, 7½-mile length of the docks was heavily damaged – notably the Wapping and Albert Docks. As well as the devastation caused at these, Huskisson No. 2 Branch Dock was obliterated when the vessel *Markland* blew up. She was carrying 1,000 tons of bombs, took a direct hit, and the resulting massive fire took seventy-four hours to burn out. An ammunition train standing in Breckside railway siding was also hit and, as it exploded, it devastated the entire district. Sections of the Overhead Railway too were bombed, disrupting dockside transport for quite a time.

Many important buildings were struck by either incendiary or high-explosive bombs, including the Customs House, India Buildings, the Corn Exchange, the Central Library, the Bluecoat Arts Centre, and the Museum. However, the work of the port had to go on; people had to live their lives; and they struggled to get to work through destroyed and rubble-strewn streets.

Throughout the war, Liverpool continued to play a strategically vital role in the defence of Britain and her Empire. From the Riverside Station (which no longer exists) at Princes Dock, 4,648 special trains carried Allied troops to and from the dockside. Indeed, no fewer than 1,747,505 servicemen and servicewomen passed through

gallant sailors have been placed at the Pier Head, together with a commemorative statue of Johnnie Walker.

Nevertheless, during the conflict more than 1,000 convoys thwarted the Germans and safely entered Liverpool, bringing with them much needed supplies of food, materials, munitions, and men. The Germans lost around 28,000 sailors in the North Atlantic, and 783 U-Boats were destroyed.

Hitler was perfectly aware of our strategic position, and so he wanted to completely obliterate Liverpool. He ordered Hermann Goering's Luftwaffe to 'bomb them into oblivion', and his air raids began in the autumn of 1940.

The first German bombs landed on Merseyside on 9 August 1940, at Prenton in Birkenhead. Then, across Merseyside, raids continued intermittently until, just before Christmas 1940, there came three nights of mass aerial bombardment. The results of these attacks left great gaps in the streets and much loss of life.

Nevertheless, the most violent aerial assault – the real Blitz – was targeted against the city during the nights of 1-8 May 1941. It was the worst week of

In the early morning of the 29 November 1940, a parachute mine was dropped on a training centre in Durning Road, in the city. In its basement, 300 men, women, and children were taking shelter from the bombing. The building collapsed, crushing many of them. Then boiling water and gas from the central heating system poured into the basement.

Fires raged overhead, making rescue work extremely dangerous and almost impossible. In all, 166 people were killed, with many more being badly injured. Winston Churchill described it as 'the single worst civilian incident of the war'.

Liverpool's Docks, on their way to and from the battlegrounds of the world. On one particular tide, there were twelve troopships queuing up in the Mersey, waiting to pick up American soldiers from the Princes Landing Stage to take them to Europe.

Children being evacuated from Britain and bound for safety in America and Canada also passed through Liverpool, and great ocean-going liners would often carry up to 2,000 of them at a time. All these transports were under constant threat of attack from the Nazi U-Boats and they all needed protection: not every ship reached their destination safely.

During the remainder of the war, the intermittent bombing raids by the Nazis that followed the Blitz, though still bad, were not as terrifying compared with those that the people had already endured. Even so, there was still much damage to property and loss of life and, between July 1940 and January 1942, the air raids on Merseyside killed 2,716 people in Liverpool, 442 people in Birkenhead, 409 people in Bootle, and 332 people in Wallasey – and injured more than 10,000 more.

However, these details were played down by the Government of the time, so as not to let the Germans know of the damage to Britain's only fully-functioning port. It has only recently been confirmed that, apart from the East End of London, Liverpool was the most heavily bombed city in Britain – in sheer weight of both high-explosive and incendiary bombs – and that we received by far the most damage of all British cities.

Liverpool took a real beating, but the spirit, courage, confidence, and sheer indomitability of Scousers, and of Merseysiders, saw us through. The city still carries the scars of the conflict on many of its buildings, and there are still one or two vacant plots of land that were bombsites. There are less and less people now who remember the bombing of Liverpool at first hand, but they continue to pass down the stories to succeeding generations. And because Britain was ultimately victorious, and Hitler's order to Goering was never fulfilled, Liverpool and Merseyside, and our proud people, survive, thrive and celebrate life!

CONCLUSION

THESE TALES OF the darker side of Liverpool's history throw a different perspective on our development as a town, and then as a city. Some are dark indeed, whilst others simply reflect the nature of the times and circumstance in which ordinary people can find themselves.

However, the incidents and personalities that I have written about are replicated, in a variety of ways, in every community in Britain: wherever there are people there is good and evil; light and shade; sources of pride and sources of shame.

But such is life; and it is through the dark times that a community and a culture learn to overcome their weaknesses, so as to progress into brighter and more optimistic times.

From that tiny, obscure fishing hamlet, on the banks of a tidal pool off a little known river, Liverpool became an engine of the Industrial Revolution; a bastion of freedom; and a defender of rights. It became a place of major achievement and a place of joy, laughter, music, and celebration.

In 2008, the city was awarded the title of European Capital of Culture, and it remains a centre of artistic, humanistic, spiritual, and community celebration. We are also a UNESCO World Heritage City and port – a further recognition of the place we have on the world stage.

In 1923, the Swiss psychologist, Carl Jung, described Liverpool as 'The Pool of Life' – for such it is. Dark times we have indeed had, and we shall no doubt have more in the future. But as we came through those we face the future with true Liverpudlian courage, determination, and good will.